CHARLES LEVER:
THE LOST VICTORIAN

CHARLES LEVER.
From a Photograph taken expressly for this Journal by Mr. C. Watkins).

A portrait of Lever produced for the *Illustrated Review,* from a photograph b
C. Watkins, taken shortly before the novelist's death on 1 June, 1872. During h
last days, Lever was visited by his friend and publisher, John Blackwood, and b
Blackwood's daughter, Mrs Gerald Porter. In *William Blackwood and His Son*
(1898), Mrs Porter gives a detailed description of their visit. Lever is buried next t
his wife, in the English Cemetery at Trieste, on Italy's Adriatic coast.

CHARLES LEVER: THE LOST VICTORIAN

STEPHEN HADDELSEY

With a Foreword by
Benedict Kiely

'The fact was, I gave the world every reasonable opportunity of knowing that they had a remarkable man amongst them, but, with a stupidity all their own, they wouldn't see it.' [1]

Copyright © 2000 by Stephen Haddelsey
Foreword copyright © 2000 by Benedict Kiely

First published in Great Britain in 2000 by Colin Smythe Ltd.
P.O. Box 6, Gerrards Cross, Buckinghamshire SL9 8XA

The right of Stephen Haddelsey to be identified as the Author
of this work has been asserted in accordance with the
Copyright, Designs and Patents Act, 1988

British Library Cataloguing in Publication Data

A catalogue record for this book
is available from the British Library

ISBN 0-86140-420-3

Distributed in North America by Oxford University Press
198 Madison Avenue, New York, NY 10016

All rights reserved. Apart from any fair dealing for the
purposes of research or private study, or criticism or review,
as permitted under the Copyright, Designs and Patents Act, 1988,
this publilcation may be reproduced, stored or transmitted,
in any forms or by any means, only with the prior permission
in writing of the publishers, or in the case of reprographic
reproduction in accordance with the terms of the licences
issued by the Copyright Licensing Agency. Enquiries
concerning reproduction outside these terms should be sent
to the publishers at the undermentioned address.

Produced in Great Britain
Printed and bound by T.J. International Ltd., Padstow, Cornwall

*For my parents
and in memory of my grandparents*

CONTENTS

FOREWORD		11
PREFACE		13
BIBLIOGRAPHICAL NOTE		15
ACKNOWLEDGMENTS		16
INTRODUCTION – WRITING ON THE MARGINS		17
1	THE NOVELS OF DR QUICKSILVER	39
2	A YEAR OF GROWTH	57
3	AN INIQUITOUS ACT	73
4	THE DOUBLE-SIDED COIN	87
5	THE ART OF BREVITY	105
6	LEVER'S ANTI-HEROINES	117
7	LAST EFFORTS	137
NOTES		155
INDEX		167

ILLUSTRATIONS

Portrait of Lever produced for the *Illustrated Review*, 1872 — *frontis*

'Trevanion astonishing the bully Gendemar.' Illustration for *The Confessions of Harry Lorrequer* (1839) by Hablot K. Browne (Phiz) — page 38

'The Reckoning.' Illustration from *The O'Donoghue* (1845) by Phiz — page 56

Half-title page to the first edition of *The Knight of Gwynne* (1847) by Phiz — page 72

'"One who never opened a cabin door without a blessing nor closed it but to shut hope within."' Illustration from *The Martins of Cro' Martin* (1856) by Phiz — page 86

between pages 96–97

Charles Lever, by Samuel Lover, engraved by H. Ryall. Frontispiece to *Jack Hinton* (1843)
Templeogue House, Dublin, towards the end of the nineteenth century, and today
William Carleton, by Charles Grey, January 29, 1843
George Whyte-Melville
William Hamilton Maxwell, by Charles Grey
Lever's chair, now in Trinity College Library, Dublin
John Blackwood, engraved by F. Huth from a photograph by Rodger
Lever, aged about forty, by Stephen Pearce

'James Dodd breaks the bank.' An illustration from *The Dodd Family Abroad* (1854) by Phiz — page 104

'"True, there is no tender light there," muttered he, gazing at her eyes,' Illustration from *Lord Kilgobbin* (1872) by Luke Fildes, R.A. — page 136

FOREWORD

The great besetting sin of this social state is the taste for notoriety. Everything must contribute to this! Not alone wealth, splendour, rank and genius, but vice, in all its shapes and forms, must be notorious. 'Better be calumniated in all the moods and tenses than be untalked of,' is the grand axiom. Do something that can be reported of you: good, if you will – bad, if you must: but do it. If you be not rich enough to astonish by the caprices of your wealth, do something by your wits, or even your whiskers. The colour of a man's gloves has sufficed to make his fortune.[1]

That's the world for you: or one aspect of it, as exactly observed and sharply commented on by Charles Lever: a man before whom I always walk in awe, as should any mortal who ever tried to write a novel or tell a story. I take that quotation at random by lifting, with my eyes closed, one volume from the vast array of his redcoated edition, done by Downey of Covent Garden, London, 1898, printed by Constable of Edinburgh, who also printed for the then Queen. And this great edition was limited to one thousand copies. So I have one edition and the present Queen may have another: and good luck to the other nine-hundred-and-ninety-eight who may possess these splendid volumes.

That random quotation I took from Volume One of *The Daltons*. And here is another, also taken at random, from the novel, *Jack Hinton: the Guardsman*:

You see that bold mountain, jagged and rugged in outline, like the spine of some gigantic beast, that runs far out into the Atlantic, and ends in a bold, abrupt headland, against which the waves, from the very coast of Labrador, are beating without one intervening rock to break their force? Carry your eye along its base, to where you can mark a little clump of alder and beech, with here and there a taper poplar interspersed, and see if you cannot detect the gable of a long, low thatched house, that lies almost buried in the foliage. Before the door a little patch of green stretches down to the shore, where a sandy beach, glowing in all the richness of a morning sun, glitters with many a shell and brilliant pebble. That, then, is Murranakilty.[2]

It would be a long, long way from Murranakilty to the world reflected in that first random quotation. But in between lies the wide world as Charles Lever saw it, understood it and wrote about it percipiently. And

Stephen Haddelsey is the most exact and eloquent guide to that wide world that I have yet encountered.

That old falsity that Lever, from a gentleman's saddle, saw the native Irish only as comic figures has long since been dismissed as the nonsense that it was. A few stern true-Gaels held it for longer than made sense. Not that it ever did. Years ago, when I was paying my respects to William Carleton, as any Tyrone man should do, I was aware that Lever and Carleton had had a brief and harmless exchange. Carleton may have been peeved as even Thackeray could have been at the best-selling splendour of Lever: it came within sight of Dickens. But out of that slight exchange Lever emerges gracefully.

He carried also a gentlemanly humour and a shrewd eye that helped him to survey the world in many places and from many angles. Stephen Haddelsey is with him all the way.

Benedict Kiely
Donnybrook
May, 1998

PREFACE

The more that one reads of Charles Lever's works, the more complex their author appears. One need only progress beyond the very earliest novels to realise just how insubstantial is the portrait painted by his Nationalist critics, both in his own time and later. Non-separatist and Tory in upbringing, by the time of his death in 1872, just short of his sixty-sixth birthday, he had moved so far from his political roots as to make the hero of his last novel, *Lord Kilgobbin*, a Fenian head-centre.

In reading his letters, it appears that his increasingly broad view of Irish politics happened almost against his will; practically to his last breath, he fulminated against Daniel O'Connell and the 'healing' measures of William Ewart Gladstone. Throughout the novels of his maturity, one discovers the author struggling to remain faithful to the tenets of his social and political education; but the struggle became increasingly unequal. In *The Martins of Cro' Martin*, for instance, his intention was to reveal the negative results of Catholic Emancipation, but by the closing chapters, the reader's sympathy is the almost exclusive preserve of the Catholic bourgeoisie which Lever had intended to ridicule; the Ascendancy Martins on the other hand – representatives of the class with whom he is most closely identified by his critics – have been exhibited as selfish, unfeeling and the victims of their own political incompetence.

During his early period of serious novel-writing, Lever was deliberately didactic. He hoped, through works such as *St Patrick's Eve*, to persuade the absentee Anglo-Irish landlords that they should return to their estates and accept their traditional duties in preserving the welfare of their tenantry. By so doing, they would become re-established as a vital component within the social framework and guarantee a future for themselves. Within a very few years, and despite the survival of an affection for and sympathy with such aristocratic landholders, his works exhibit a hopeless recognition not only that the 'old-order' would never be re-established, but that its failure was almost exclusively the fault of the Ascendancy itself.

Even today, one can pick up literary reference books, flick to the passage on Lever, and find him allocated to the 'huntin', shootin', fishin'' school of literature, along with Surtees and Ouida: cheerful, devil-may-care and essentially lightweight. The fact is, however, that *Harry Lorrequer* and *Charles O'Malley* aside, his novels are marked deeply by gloom and pessimism. There is humour in all his works, usually to be found in his rich and varied exploration of character, but the more he wrote of the condition of Ireland from his vantage point on the Continent, the more he became convinced not only that the Ascendancy was a dying breed, but that an all-encompassing accord might never prove possible; certainly that it could never be engineered by the blinkered and blundering Castle administration.

In the novels there is many a rich vein yet to be mined by Irish or international critics. Lever's place as a Europeanised Irish novelist and the influences of Scott and Balzac; his sympathetic but wholly unidealised analysis of the restricted role allocated to women in Victorian society; his importance as a military novelist. In this short book, I have touched on each of these and a number of other subjects, but there is much more that might yet be said. The current lack of modern texts means that critics and readers alike will have to trawl through the shelves of second-hand and antiquarian bookshops – but, then, who knows what other worthies might thereby spring into the light?

BIBLIOGRAPHICAL NOTE

The editions of Lever's works published during the nineteenth century are manifold. Of *Charles O'Malley* alone, no fewer than forty-one editions were published in England and the United States between 1841 and 1899, with a further fifteen editions being published by 1947. There is, however, no modern edition of any of his novels, with the exception of *Lord Kilgobbin*, which was published as recently as 1992 by the Appletree Press of Belfast.

By far the most valuable, is *The Copyright Edition of the Novels of Charles Lever* published by Downey and Company (1897-99). However, this edition – in thirty-six volumes – remains rare and, to the purchaser, expensive. For this reason, the majority of the references to Lever's novels throughout the text have been standardised to the more accessible Routledge edition (undated, but c.1890).

The standard biographical sources remain:

Edmund Downey, *Charles Lever: his life in his letters*, 2 vols. (Edinburgh and London: William Blackwood and Sons, 1906).

W.J. Fitzpatrick, *The Life of Charles Lever*, [new revised edition]. (London: Ward, Lock and Co., 1884).

Lionel Stevenson, *Dr Quicksilver: the Life of Charles Lever*. (London: Chapman and Hall, 1939).

ACKNOWLEDGMENTS

I should like to thank my wife, Bernadette, for her constant encouragement and enthusiasm during the research and writing of this volume; Bob Hudson for his academic criticism; Andrew Stevenson for his skill in designing the cover graphics; and my Father for his Herculean struggles with PCs and printers.

Most of all, I should like to express my appreciation to my brother, Martin, my sternest and most committed critic; and to Benedict Kiely, not only for his generous Foreword, but for his unflagging kindness in supporting this project.

Stephen Haddelsey
Southwell
August, 1998

INTRODUCTION –

WRITING ON THE MARGINS

– I –

In the early 1840s, Charles James Lever was at the peak of his popularity. With the publication of his second novel, *Charles O'Malley*, in 1841, he had established himself as one of Britain's most sought-after writers. Applauded by a public seemingly ravenous for the easy-going, rollicking and essentially undisciplined fictions which he could produce with such facility, he also enjoyed an abundance of laudatory critical notices which frequently compared him favourably with his main rival, Charles Dickens:

> It is not easy to say what might have been the relevant positions of *Lorrequer* and *Pickwick*, had the former preceded instead of following [sic] Mr Dickens' work. The author of *Lorrequer* is a person of equal buoyancy of spirits, of more extended observation, and not inferior in vigour of fancy and description.[1]

Considered to be in the vanguard of the new generation of up-and-coming young novelists, Lever had become the darling of publishers with an eye to the main chance. Almost single-handedly, his contributions had made the fortunes of the *Dublin University Magazine*, founded in 1833 by Isaac Butt. By January 1846, when he began work on his eighth novel, *The Knight of Gwynne*, he could command sums on a par with those demanded by Dickens and far in excess of any earned by writers such as Thackeray:

> The terms were munificent: £130 a monthly number, a sliding provision extending from a minimum of twelve to 'twenty or any less quantity of numbers'. The likely reward for Lever, £2,000 or more, was a sum previously given only to Dickens . . . Chapman and Hall also planned production on a Dickensian scale. Ten thousand copies of the first monthly number were budgeted for, with the option of an extra £10 to Lever for each thousand additional to the initial figure.[2]

Unfortunately, as J.A. Sutherland describes, *The Knight of Gwynne* 'came to an end amid a general feeling of gloom and mortification'.[3]

With the novel's commencement, Lever's career had achieved its zenith. After its conclusion, he would never again reach the same expansive audience or reap such magnificent financial rewards.

Within a few months of his death, he began a series of new prefaces to his novels. That to *Harry Lorrequer* (1839) bears testimony both to his youthful elation when he learned of his astounding early success but also, more poignantly, to his later feelings of melancholy and uncertainty over whether he had followed the right course in abandoning the security and respectability of his medical career:

> I suppose I am only admitting what many others under like circumstances might declare, that I have had my moments, and more than mere moments, of doubt and misgiving that I have made the wiser choice, and bating the intense pleasure an occasional success has afforded, I have been led to think that the career I had abandoned would have been more rewarding, more safe from reverses, and less exposed to those variations of public taste which are the terrors of all who live on the world's favour.[4]

What was the exact nature of these reverses? What was it that resulted in a marginalisation so pronounced as to become, virtually, a total exclusion? How was it that the only nineteenth century Irish novelist to vie with Dickens in popularity and earning power, whose name – during his early career – was a household word, could become within fifty years of his death almost completely unknown?

– II –

As Dr Sutherland has indicated in his analysis of the failure of *The Knight of Gwynne*, external events were perhaps as decisive in Lever's fall from favour as any change in style or subject:

> Unforeseen factors hurt the novel. The cover, for instance, displayed Ireland 'GREAT, GLORIOUS AND FREE', with vignettes recording the country's progress 'in the development of her resources in the happiness of her people from Poverty, Misery and Anarchy'. It was cruel luck that the work should have coincided with the potato famine which starved Ireland's population and plunged the country into a misery, poverty and anarchy unequalled in modern times.[5]

As we have seen, his Irish background apparently presented no hindrance to the success of his comic early works with an English audience. Admittedly, there was little in the first novels which might be considered offensive by such readers: two of his three most popular heroes, Harry Lorrequer and Jack Hinton, are English, whilst the third, Charles O'Malley, is the son of an ancient and feckless family, of a kind first introduced by Maria Edgeworth in *Castle Rackrent* (1800). They are the

Introduction – Writing on the Margins

fictional heirs of the previous century's Tom Jones and Perigrine Pickle, although their antics are performed, for the most part, on Irish rather than English soil. Even his more deliberately 'Irish' novels, *St Patrick's Eve* (1845) and *The O'Donoghue* (1845) produced no immediately noticeable diminution in his readership, though their subject matter included both the appalling aftermath of the Clare cholera epidemic of 1832 and the dispossession of the traditional nobility by the invading Englishman. The first of the blows which shattered Lever's popularity was the coinciding of his deliberate attempt to develop his writing style with the most devastating natural calamity to strike modern Ireland. Irish subject matter suddenly became too uncomfortable a read for an English audience, and for an author who was already revealing a strong inclination towards more serious material whilst at the same time refusing to abandon either Irish heroes or Irish stories, their desertion spelled near disaster. Simultaneous with his efforts to broaden his sphere of interest and to appeal to an altogether different class of reader from that which took his rowdy picaresque heroes to its bosom, the ambitious novelist found himself effectively beached with the tide of public favour rapidly retreating. Those efforts which should have brought him at least a retrospective critical reappraisal, were almost universally ignored and the immature and boisterous essays at popular authorship, instead of being eclipsed by his serious and often topical later novels, remained in the public and critical consciousness, fuelling an almost painfully unrevisionist condemnation. Joseph Sheridan Le Fanu, a generation younger than Lever, would not make the same mistake, and though he criticised his English readers for their prejudice and remained resident in Ireland, he bowed before the pressure resisted by Lever and was 'eventually pushed . . . into setting his novels in England and Wales'.[6] Ironically, it is the writer who yielded to these demands whose works have enjoyed a revival of popular interest in the twentieth century – spurred largely by M.R. James's championship of his short stories in the 1920s. Lever, on the other hand, has never been allowed to step from beneath the shadow of his first, most obviously Anglophone works.

Although he has often been classed as an Ascendancy writer, Lever's background was rather more humble: his father, James, was a successful builder and architect while his mother was descended from Cromwellian settlers (an inheritance which, Edmund Downey points out, was shared by Thomas Davis). He was educated in various schools for the scions of middle-class houses and graduated from Trinity in 1827. Many aspects of the early novels can be ascribed to actual experience – their rich fund of military anecdote, for instance, was certainly a product of the author's acquaintance with the retired British officers resident in Brussels – but his initial choice of upper-class hero was perhaps more a product of fashionable literary trends than a reflection of his everyday social commerce. Not that fashion was the only force at work; in the first instance, his choice of Ascendancy hero may well have been influenced by the novels of Maria Edgeworth, Lady Morgan and Sir Walter Scott, but his career provides ample evidence of an enduring fascination with the impecunious squirearchy of Ireland.

From *Charles O'Malley* (1841) to *Lord Kilgobbin* (1872), Lever would return periodically to the sometimes boisterous but invariably mortgaged squireens and to what J.M. Synge described as 'the tragedy of the landlord class . . . and of the innumerable old families that are quickly dwindling away'.[7] Despite this affection, however, his attitude towards the Ascendancy was both complex and subject to change and his analysis of its characteristics and motivations became progressively more sensitive and critical. A. Norman Jeffares has identified Sir Walter Scott's influence on Lever, drawing particular attention to his rather long-winded, set-piece introductions to his novels.[8] Another parallel might be drawn between the criticism levelled at Scott for his choice of aristocratic heroes and that directed at Lever for his decision to create Ascendancy protagonists. The defence of Scott offered by the Marxist critic, Georg Lukacs, might also be utilised in the Irishman's favour:

Scott very often shows in a humorous, satirical or tragic manner the weakness, the human and moral degeneration of the upper strata . . . the chief tendency in their portrayal is to show their inability to fulfil their historic missions.[9]

The novels of Lever's middle and later periods demonstrate precisely this tendency and form a stark contrast to the earlier works which 'exemplify the Ascendancy laughing at itself'.[10] In contemporary accounts written from the Ascendancy point of view, R.F. Foster has identified what might be described as a selective race memory, a recollection of 'a lost Golden Age of good relations between landlord and tenant, Protestant and Catholic'.[11] This same wistfulness can be found in certain of Lever's works, for instance in the otherwise cruelly realistic *St Patrick's Eve* when the story concludes with the new landlord's fresh acceptance of his responsibility towards his tenants. In the later, and gloomier, *The Martins of Cro' Martin* (1856), however, such a rosy solution is tantalisingly offered and then snatched away, its plausibility denied. In this novel Lever voices much of his reluctant realism through the mouth of the crusty barrister Valentine Repton who at one point declares, 'Ireland is not to be redeemed by her own gentry. The thing is sheer impossibility!'.[12] Lever never abandoned his belief in the one-time existence of a two-way contract, the interdependence of landlord and tenant, but by the late 1850s he accepted that any return to such a system was no longer practicable. Another facet of this novel is his recognition that the conflict is not restricted to a simple black-and-white confrontation between aristocratic landlord and peasant. The tensions produced by the rise of an independent, educated Catholic bourgeoisie are also identified and analysed, with his initial cynicism with regard to the motivations of such small town entrepreneurs gradually being replaced by a grudging respect.

In an earlier novel, *The O'Donoghue*, Lever had also refuted the suggestion that the problems of rural Ireland could be solved by the introduction of new landlords. At the story's commencement we witness the arrival of Sir Marmaduke Travers who has purchased the estate of the impoverished O'Donoghue family. He immediately sets about the implementation of new schemes to enrich the land, but his good intentions are crippled by his own narrow-mindedness and arrogance:

Had he taken but one-half the pains to learn something of national character that he bestowed on his absurd efforts to fashion it to his liking, his success might have been different.[13]

Travers is, in fact, a representative of the blinkered, incompetent and self-opinionated English administration which Lever deplored. His outspokenness on the subject is further evidence of his unwillingness to deny the complexity of Ireland's problems. Nor would he subscribe to the popular theory that a brief sojourn in Ireland was the only prerequisite for a sympathetic appreciation of the country's predicament; an over-simplification which became prevalent in early Anglo-Irish fiction. A great admirer of Maria Edgeworth – whose didactic novel *Ennui* (1809) was the first in this genre – he did produce one work in this optimistic vein, *Jack Hinton* (1843), but, as a rule, his other novels, as disparate in tone and style as *Harry Lorrequer* and *Lord Kilgobbin*, emphasise the imperviousness of most English visitors to any real sympathy with or understanding of things Irish. Increasingly, as his conviction of the impossibility of political and social cohesion grew, his tone became despairing.

One of Lever's greatest strengths as a novelist was his refusal to become 'boxed' and associated with any one creed; not for him the belief that:

the memory of homeland has to be kept in aspic. The perspective over one's shoulder must remain identical to that recorded by the parting glance – even if that moment happened two (or more) generations back, and even if the remembered impression is spectacularly contradicted by the mother country itself as experienced on return visits.[14]

Professor Foster makes specific reference to the *émigré's* 'cultural insecurity', the need in the face of severance from one's homeland to retain a crystal-clear and immutable image of it. Lever is an exception to this rule, despite the fact that he spent the second half of his life on the Continent, returning to Ireland only briefly and irregularly. For him, separation engendered not a restrictive nostalgia but rather an objectivity which enabled him, in *Lord Kilgobbin*, to portray sympathetically the Fenian Daniel Donogan, the traditional enemy of both his Toryism and Unionism. This attitude is perhaps even more remarkable in that it is exhibited most potently in the last of his novels, where an inclination toward nostalgia might be more sympathetically regarded by even his harshest critics. Instead of allowing himself the opportunity to create a 'Golden Age' through the medium of an historical novel, he created one of his most determinedly contemporary stories in which the Fenian risings, Home Rule and the disestablishment of the Church of Ireland all see their faces darkly reflected in the mirror of fiction.

With maturity Lever became more liberal in his outlook, but even in his early period of 'serious' novel writing he had shown a willingness to offend the sensibilities of his own party. His freedom in novels such as *The O'Donoghue* and in the essays of *Nuts and Nutcrackers* (1845) resulted in his weathering a storm of criticism from the Tory readership of the *Dublin University Magazine*, and perhaps reveals a willingness to accept or even to court unconsciously a marginalisation which he bemoaned on a number of occasions. In his full and fascinating essay on 'Lever and the Outsider', Tony Bareham has investigated Lever's apparent obsession with those characters who experience some form of exclusion and has drawn comparisons with the author's own life:

> The career of Charles Lever suggests very strongly a man striving to be at the centre of things, but constantly being impelled towards the periphery, a position of 'outsiderness'. This tendency is manifest both in the biography and in the fiction.[15]

Certainly it is tempting to see his current exclusion from the established literary canon as in some part a reflection of his feelings of separation during his life, and in some part, perhaps, as the direct result of them – particularly in terms of his decision to choose 'difficult' subject matter. Whether or not, as Professor Bareham suggests, Lever's marginalisation was the result of some unconscious impulse, it was productive not only of negatives. In his examination of the role of the outsider, for instance:

Probably no other mid-Victorian novelist develops the theme of outsiderness more broadly or comprehensively or makes this character-type so consistently the focus of his attention.[16]

His own unusual position of 'outsiderness' enabled him to survey developments in Ireland with a critical objectivity perhaps lacking in other contemporary accounts. One of the attractions of popular literature may be its capacity to confirm us in our own view of the world; it offers a tantalising aestheticisation of the normal. If this is the case, the objectivity born of Lever's geographical separation, which enabled him to offer fresh and dynamic views of Irish affairs, may have been responsible in part for an exclusion from the affections of a reading public which preferred to have its prejudices flattered.

He appears to have been consumed by a wander-lust which precluded any lengthy residence in Ireland, although it is highly unlikely that he was motivated by the same artistic aspirations later articulated by George Bernard Shaw:

Every Irishman who felt that his business in life was on the higher planes of the cultural professions felt that he must have a metropolitan domicile and an international culture: that is, he felt that his first business was to get out of Ireland.[17]

The immediate catalyst for Lever's departure from Ireland was a conversation held with Thackeray during the latter's visit to Templeogue House, as recorded in *The Irish Sketchbook* (1843), which was dedicated to Lever. Thackeray encouraged his host to transfer his residence to the bustling literary centre of London and to thereby avoid the risk of 'provincialisation'. Instead, he resigned his editorship of the *Dublin University Magazine*, his tenure of which had become increasingly uncomfortable as a result of political squabbling, and took his family to the Continent, and to years of peripatetic uncertainty. His knowledge of mainland Europe is evidenced increasingly throughout his works, but the heroes of even his earliest novels tread, at some point, the soil of Europe: *Harry Lorrequer* concludes in Munich, while *Charles O'Malley* is largely concerned with the eponymous hero's adventures in the Peninsula Campaigns. Although the decision to move away from Ireland and from England was his own, on a number of occasions Lever pathetically bemoaned his existence on the fringe; on a trip to London in May 1856, for example, he declared:

It is sheer madness for any man who has to live by his brains to be removed from this great market. I can see now how recklessly I have played my cards, this life, and if I had settled down here I should have been a rich man to-day.[18]

Yet it was this self-imposed exile and his concomitant role as a Europeanised Irishman which make him almost unique in the nineteenth century. In novels as widely separated as *The Martins of Cro' Martin* and *Lord Kilgobbin* we find the condition of Ireland viewed if not from an entirely European perspective, then at least from a perspective in which patriotic warmth is tempered by Continental objectivity. In the earlier of the two novels, for instance, Lever actually uses the French revolution of 1830 and the dethronement of Charles X to forecast the inevitable downfall of the landlord system in Ireland. In his only mature essay at comedy, *The Dodd Family Abroad* (1854), he utilises the hilarious misunderstandings of the travelling Dodds to shape a lesson on how the Irish and English might come to better understand their neighbours across the English Channel. Having dwelt at different periods of his life in Belgium, Germany and Italy (as well as a youthful excursion into Canada, if his early and perhaps apocryphal biography is to be believed), he speaks with the conviction of experience and in adopting a wide canvas, both geographically and socially, he does not extend beyond his personal knowledge of the world. In his introduction to *Lord Kilgobbin*, A. Norman Jeffares summarises this breadth of vision and his comments have an equal relevance to the gamut of Lever's mature works:

He knows very well the different worlds he brings together in his novels . . .

The novel is spacious in more than setting: its social range spans the gulf between Irish and English sensibilities while adding in the continental element. [19]

In describing how 'living between Ireland and Britain . . . was sometimes an enabling experience',[20] R.F. Foster makes specific reference to 'the extraordinary record of Irish literature in the English language'. A. Norman Jeffares describes the creative tensions resulting from this dual inheritance as 'Janus-like',[21] but, in the case of Lever, this analysis can be taken a step further since he was, exceptionally, caught between not two cultures, but three: and, as with the particular cases cited by Professor Foster, the experience was, perhaps, disorienting but also, ultimately, 'enabling'.

With this wealth of experience, which is given such rich expression in his novels, how is it that so much attention has been lavished on Lever's immature solecisms? *Harry Lorrequer* and *Charles O'Malley* simultaneously made and blasted his reputation: it was these novels and their immediate successors in the same genre which established him as a popular novelist and which also attracted the adverse criticism of William Carleton and other Nationalists. When Yeats wrote of him that he had 'caught the ear of the world and come to stand for the entire nation',[22] he referred to these early works, and it was to them that he pointed when he repeated Carleton's attack. Anthony Trollope who, in

Introduction – Writing on the Margins

his *Autobiography*, described Lever as his 'dear old friend' and accorded him a position among the successful novelists of his own time, went on to state confidently that 'his novels will not live long', while also admitting that he had not read any of the later ones.[23] Even the impartial nineteenth century English critic, George Saintsbury, whose choice was certainly not driven by any hidden Nationalist agenda, cites *Charles O'Malley* as Lever's 'masterpiece'.[24] It was the immediate and widespread fame of the early novels, their command of such a numerous audience, which made it worthwhile for Carleton to point out their demerits; once Lever had slipped from his pinnacle, however, his novels attracted less high-profile attention. Certainly it is tempting, though ultimately futile, to conjecture what process of ongoing critical reappraisal he would have enjoyed if his later works had topped the best-seller lists in the same manner as the earliest. One would like to believe that if *Lord Kilgobbin* had received the same attention as *Harry Lorrequer*, from both readers and critics, we would be far less likely to find modern critical authorities of Declan Kiberd's weight rolling out the tired old clichés concerning Lever's supposed predilection for the 'stage Irishman'.[25] But we must also consider the influence on Lever's reputation of prevalent attitudes toward the Anglo-Irish.

In February 1994, during an edition of RTE's *The Arts Show*, Chris Morash succinctly described the predicament of many nineteenth century Anglo-Irish authors, though he referred specifically to Lever and to his near contemporary, Samuel Lover:

> They were too Irish for an English canon but they were too English for an Irish canon, and, as a result, they fell somewhere into the Irish Sea – and that's where they've been floundering around ever since.[26]

In traditional Nationalist consciousness, an Anglo-Irish heritage has been almost synonymous with exclusion. In this narrow view of a complex situation, Loyalism totemically represents cultural imperialism, the incursion of outside forces which threaten to undermine some 'essential' notion of Irishness. Only those Anglo-Irish writers of the very first rank have been able to erase the brand, without simultaneously denying their cultural roots:

> Then I remind myself that though mine is the first English marriage I know of in the direct line, all my family names are English; that I owe my soul to Shakespeare, to Spenser, to Blake . . . and to the English language in which I think, speak and write; that everything I love has come to me through English.[27]

It is unlikely that Lever would have felt the need to make a confession as theatrical as Yeats's. The son of an English immigrant father and an Irish mother; a Tory, a Protestant and a Unionist, he considered himself, above all things, an Irishman. Yeats's sense of being torn between two traditions was a later development, consequent on the growing tension between Ireland and the 'mainland'. So far as Lever was concerned, 'Irishness' was not an absolute, susceptible to some grand, all-encompassing definition which rigorously excluded certain forms of experience. In the passionate introduction to his incisive study *Paddy and Mr Punch*, R.F. Foster sensitively plots this ground, inhabited by so many of the Anglo-Irish and those '"caught", between the two countries':

cultural diversity and cross-channel borrowings are implicit in Irish history, and cannot be denied by piety or suppressed by violence. The way people saw themselves as Irish deserves more attention than the awarding or denying of Irishness as a mark of good conduct, or embarking on self-justifying searches for uncorrupted 'roots', or taking refuge in self-congratulatory conspiracy theories.[28]

Having asserted that '"Victorian Ireland" could be middle class, English-speaking and non-separatist in its politics, but no less "Irish" for that',[29] Professor Foster goes on to posit the theory that the mere habitation of Ireland 'imposes its own common bonds, and that these coexist with different cultural, religious and even political traditions'.[30] Such liberal and non-sectarian values, however, ill-accord with the rhetoric of Nationalist historians such as Daniel Corkery, author of *The Hidden Ireland* (1924), who advocated the Gaelic exclusivity of Irish culture and denied Anglo-Irish writings a place in the national literature. The adoption of the traditional Nationalist creed has involved the exclusion of all things Anglo-Irish as abortive grafts onto the pure Gaelic culture of Ireland and Lever was undoubtedly seen as a representative of this cultural imperialism. Without citing any of his works, Professor Foster lists a number of novels written by nineteenth century Anglo-Irish authors, and asks:

Can it be a coincidence that all of these texts were banished from the supposedly authentic canon of Irish literature by the exclusivist version of Irish culture peddled by Daniel Corkery?[31]

Emphasis is placed on Lever's infrequent portrayals of peasant life because it is this side of Irish life which has been glorified by Nationalist historians and critics. By the same token, Ascendancy and middle class existence has been deliberately marginalised and either obscured or denigrated by the pastoralist Gaelic League, with its avowedly Nationalist agenda and idealised vision of a Celtic civilisation in the west. Similar modes of thought lay behind Karl Marx's dismissive reference to Lever

Introduction – Writing on the Margins 27

in his analysis of Carleton's work: 'As the son of an Irish peasant he knows his subject better than the Levers and Lovers';[32] the important thing here is not so much Marx's failure to understand Lever's subject matter but his insistence that it is the peasant and rural existence which are the only important subjects. In any such climate the reputation of an artist like Lever must suffer, not simply because he was predominantly concerned with these excluded forms of existence but also because he was, in essence, little concerned with peasant life. Although they are discussed in much greater detail later in this book, it can be noted here that in novels such as *St Patrick's Eve* and *The Martins of Cro' Martin* his depictions of the peasantry tend to be innocent of either the sentimentality or the humour-inclined condescension more reasonably ascribed to writers like Samuel Lover. In fact, they are founded on the knowledge gained during his attendance upon such communities during the cholera epidemic of the early 1830s. Aware of the English predilection for the supposed 'quaintness' of Irish life and perhaps also feeling pangs of guilt for any concession which he may once have made to such demands, in *The Martins of Cro' Martin*, and once more using Valentine Repton as his acerbic mouthpiece, Lever declares:

'as a maxim, sir, remember, that the inhabitants of a country are never so much to be pitied as when the aspect of their social condition is picturesque!'[33]

It is also worthwhile to note that on the one commonly quoted occasion on which he found himself harshly criticised for a burlesque portrayal of the peasantry, his reaction was not to dismiss or to defend but rather to reappraise his work and to redirect it.

– III –

In its contribution to the predominantly laudatory obituaries published after Lever's death on 1 June 1872, the *Observer* claimed that:

amidst all the reckless extravagance, the uproarious humour and brilliant slap-dash, they read between the lines of *Lorrequer* a power of description, an insight into character, a mine of thought which one might look for in vain in works of far higher pretensions. [34]

Although we might reasonably dispute the obituarist's decision to retrospectively endow Lever's first novel with the qualities of his mature fiction, the summary has a value in that it identifies characterisation and description as two of his chief abilities.

The *Dictionary of National Biography* described his characters as 'generally transcripts from the life' and Thackeray, among others, laughed at his inability to resist the temptation to portray those with whom he mingled socially. Whether Thackeray was quite so amused at his own portrayal as Elias Howle in *Roland Cashel*[35] is not recorded, though any overly critical attitude would have been rather hypocritical since he almost certainly used Lever as his model for the creation of Shannon, the impecunious Irish hack in *Pendennis*. Lever apparently saw no reason to apologise for his habit and openly admitted to using his acquaintances in his books. Two well known examples are the originals of Colonel Kamworth in *Harry Lorrequer* and Major Monsoon in *Charles O'Malley*. In his preface to the latter novel he boldly stated:

That certain traits of my acquaintances found themselves embodied in some of the characters in this story, I do not seek to deny.[36]

The habit may have been formed early in his career but it would be a mistake to think that he relied solely upon this resource, or to believe that he was incapable or unwilling to build and expand his creations beyond their factual base. As his use of the phrase 'certain traits' indicates, in the vast majority of cases it was select characteristics, rather than complete personas, which he borrowed. An example of this creative response to historical fact in a mature fiction can be located in *The Martins of Cro' Martin*. Despite his firm denial that his heroine, Mary Martin, was based upon Mary Letitia Martin, the similarities in name and in their histories – as identified by Chris Morash – would seem to refute this claim. Whether these similarities were deliberate or unconscious, our attention should focus on the significant divergence of fiction from fact:

There is . . . a major difference between the fictional Mary Martin and her non-fictional counterpart. At the end of *The Martins of Cro' Martin*, as it becomes apparent that the estate is destined to be broken up by the Encumbered Estates Court, Mary Martin dies, surrounded by the mourning peasantry to whom she had devoted her life. Mary Letitia Martin, after equally exhausting efforts during the 1840s, found herself in 1848 the mistress of an equally bankrupt estate. She, however, did not die a tearful romantic death. She, like Charles Lever, emigrated to Belgium, where she wrote novels dealing with the fall of the Irish Big House.[37]

The same flexible approach, the same imaginative blending of fact and fancy, can be found in his treatment of landscape and architecture. In *The Bramleighs of Bishop's Folly* (1868), for instance, the house in which much of the action takes place, the 'Bishop's Folly', was, as Lionel Stevenson states, 'suggested by "Downhill", the vast Italianate palace which had been built on a bleak headland opposite Portstewart by the eccentric Earl of Bristol who was also Bishop of Derry'.[38] However, the location of the house is changed in the novel and it is transferred 'lock, stock and barrel to County Down'.[39]

It is not in the author's willingness to tinker with geography and character that the most important links between landscape description and characterisation are to be found, rather it is in his use of the one to examine and comment upon the other. As a number of his more recent critics have indicated, there can be found a definite correlation between his use of description – most particularly landscape and architectural description – and his treatment of character:

> Lever handles descriptions of landscape with dexterity and sensitivity, across a wide range of types of scenery. The validity of his geography underpins his observation of character.[40]

Throughout his mature fiction, beginning as early as *The O'Donoghue*, Lever used the one to highlight the other, and to define social position with great subtlety. This ability is particularly pertinent to his analysis of Irish society in which varied forms of marginalisation and exclusion are apparent: English interlopers from the indigenous population; Catholic landlords from governance; and Ascendancy landlords from their tenantry.

The Bramleighs of Bishop's Folly is an example of Lever using a building and its location as a yardstick with which to measure the standing of its inhabitants. The 'Folly' is an architectural misfit, standing apart from its neighbours in exactly the same manner in which the interloping English Bramleighs remain segregated from theirs. Furthermore, it is made clear from the very first pages of the novel that their decision to take up residence, to restore the house's former glories and to further aggrandise it with the name 'Castello', will have little or no lasting impact: 'It was Bishop's Folly when I was a boy, and it will be Bishop's Folly after I'm dead'.[41] A similar process of unspoken comparative analysis is used in other novels, most noticeably *The Martins of Cro' Martin*, *Lord Kilgobbin* and *Sir Brook Fossbrooke* (1866). Unusually, in the last of these novels, the house in which much of the action takes place, the home of Baron Lendrick, alters its appearance as its possessor alters his:

> We are once more at the Priory – but how changed is it all! Billy Haire himself scarcely recognises the old spot, and, indeed, comes now but seldom to visit it . . .
> The old elm under whose shade Avonmore and the wits used to sit of an evening, beneath whose leafy canopy Curran had jested and Moore had sung, was cut down, and a large tent of gaudy blue and white spread its vulgar wings over innumerable breakfast tables, set forth with what the newspapers call every delicacy of the season . . .
> Of the wild old woodland walks – shady and cool, redolent of sweet briar and

honeysuckle – not a trace remains; driving-roads, wide enough for a pony-carriage, have been substituted for these, and ruthless gaps in the dense wood open long vistas to the eye, in a spot where once it was the sense of enclosure and seclusion that imparted the chief charm . . . But of all the changes and mutations which a short time had effected, none could compete with that in the old Chief himself.[42]

The transformations in the Priory and its garden reinforce the impact of the Baron's foolish adoption of undignified fopperies; the destruction of the 'old woodland walks' provides an exact corollary to his decision to don 'a light-brown wig' and face-paint. This development in *Sir Brook Fossbrooke* is exceptional, in that the commentary provided through architecture in the other cited novels exemplifies permanence, either of exclusion, in *The Martins of Cro' Martin*, or of decay, in *The O'Donoghue*, or of both, in *Lord Kilgobbin*. The alterations wrought in the fabric of the Priory and its demesne are instead used to illustrate mutability both in Man and in his surroundings.

Lever's landscape descriptions are remarkable not only for their subtle reinforcement of character traits. In many cases they have a power and beauty which is their own justification. Moreover, as Chris Morash has pointed out:

he was able to recall the landscapes of Ireland with a vividness that suggests an almost Joycean effort of memory. Indeed, like Joyce, the longer he spent living in exile the more lengthy and the more detailed his descriptions of Ireland became.[43]

The earliest novels pay little heed to scenery, save where topography is relevant to military strategy, but the later works written in exile contain extensive passages of landscape description. A. Norman Jeffares has attributed Lever's attention to scenery to the influence of Sir Walter Scott[44] but we might also consider other unconscious and quintessentially Irish influences which Nationalist critics might feel inclined to deny to Lever:

The personification and highly charged nature of the Irish response to the land is, of course, a tradition in Gaelic literature . . . The Irish identification with the land, its unique appearance, its light and shade, also owes much to English-derived romanticism . . . And this might indicate that such perceptions can be reconciling and unifying too.[45]

If a Nationalist doctrine of Anglo-Irish marginalisation still exists, then its exponents will object as strongly to this linking of Lever's name to a Gaelic tradition as to James M. Cahalan's attribution of his early anecdotal fiction to the influence of the indigenous tradition of oral storytelling,[46] thereby denying any hopes for reconciliation and unification.

In his discussion of 'English-derived romanticism', Professor Foster makes specific reference to Wordsworth, and the influence of the English poet can be discerned, perhaps, in certain of Lever's descriptive passages; in *That Boy of Norcott's* (1869), for instance, we find the following:

> The scene itself was of rare beauty. Seated as I was, the bay appeared a vast lake, for the outlet that led seaward was backed by an island, and thus the coast-line seemed unbroken throughout. Over this wide expanse now hundreds of fishing boats were moving in every direction, for the wind was blowing fresh from the land, and permitted them to tack and beat as they pleased. If thus in the crisply curling waves, the flitting boats, and the fast-flying clouds above, there was motion and life, there was, in the high-peaked mountain that frowned above me, and in the dark rocks that lined the shore, a stern, impressive grandeur that became all the more striking from contrast. The plashing water, the fishermen's cries, the merry laughter of the revellers as they strayed through break and copse, seemed all but whispering sounds in that vast amphitheatre of mountain, so solemn was the influence of those towering crags that rose towards heaven.[47]

If *The Excursion* seems to lurk behind these lines, there is nothing in this presence which denies the 'Irishness' of Lever's landscape appreciation. Yeats admitted the influence of Scott, Blake, Macauley and Shakespeare and there was nothing in the confession which nullified the impact of Ireland on his consciousness. By the time Lever wrote *Lord Kilgobbin*, he was able to offer the contention that landscape and nationalism were intrinsically linked and, furthermore, to comment upon the English perception that this bond was particularly strong in Ireland:

> 'With half a dozen days like this,' said Atlee, as he smoked his cigarette, in a sort of languid grace, 'one would not say O'Connell was wrong in his glowing admiration for Irish scenery. If I were to wake every day for a week to this, I suspect I should grow somewhat crazy myself about the green island.'
> 'And dash the description with a little treason too,' said the other superciliously. 'I have always remarked the ingenious connection with which Irishmen bind up a love of the picturesque with a hate of the Saxon.'[48]

The manner in which landscape, particularly Irish landscape, became increasingly important in Lever's novels has been described already and will be addressed again in later chapters, but it is worthwhile, here, to highlight again how his long residence outside Ireland enabled him not only to describe his native country with freshness and an analytical shrewdness but also to bring the benefits of a peculiarly Irish tradition to his descriptions of the face, as well as the character, of Europe.

– IV –

Having produced no fewer than thirty novels and five collections of essays in a writing career spanning approximately thirty-five years, Lever is often criticised for over-production. Realistically, any attempt to refute the accusation is doomed to failure, even though his output was much lower than Trollope's and amounted to only one third the total of that most prolific of Victorian novelists, G.P.R. James. In many ways he was typical of nineteenth century authorship and it is, therefore, appropriate to consider the conditions in which he worked.

Almost all of his fiction was written for publication in the form of monthly parts, the parts would then be gathered together and reissued in volume form. This method of production, which was revived by Dickens with the publishers Chapman and Hall after a break of some fifty years, was ideally suited to Lever's methods of composition, having, as he admitted to Maria Edgeworth, 'no constructiveness in my head'. In his comprehensive study of the influence of Victorian publishers on their authors, J.A. Sutherland has described the kind of novels which such practices produced:

> The reader had the fiction, as the phrase went, 'warm from the brain' and usually before any critical judgement could be imposed on it, giving the work a singular freshness.[49]

Harry Lorrequer and *Charles O'Malley* certainly abound with this 'freshness', indeed it is often considered to be their greatest and, all too often, their only merit. Lever's letters and biographies are filled with tales of rushed composition and instalments lost in the European postal network; as Tony Bareham states, he 'never wrote a single book which was completed before the dispatch of individual episodes to the printer'.[50] In his last introduction to *Harry Lorrequer*, Lever recounted how the published conclusion to the novel was in fact quite different from the one which he had originally written, and explained why:

> The MSS. which contained the conclusion of the story had been sent through the Foreign Office bag from Brussels, and possibly had been mistaken for a dispatch. At all events, like King Theodore's letter, it had been thrown to one side and forgotten. In this strait my publishers wrote to me in a strain that the trade alone knows how to employ towards an unknown author.
> Stung by the reproaches . . . of my correspondent, I wrote back, enclosing another conclusion, and telling him to print either or both – as he pleased. Years after, I saw the first sent MSS . . . bound in my publisher's library, and lettered 'Another ending to H.L.'[51]

In fairness, it should be stated that he prefaced this story with a retrospective criticism of his failure to understand 'the responsibilities of authorship'. Having first taken up his pen in an attempt to pay off debts accumulated at the whist table, gambling losses remained an important motivation and in 1863 he admitted to writing 'from hand to mouth'.

Of course, the gambling aside, there was nothing unusual in Lever's

Introduction – Writing on the Margins

rushed and essentially chaotic mode of composition. He was just one of the many authors who toiled in what J.A. Sutherland has described as 'the furnace-like conditions in which much of the best Victorian fiction was created'.[52] The errors in continuity, the implausible coincidences of plot, the huddled endings: all are to be found in the works of the greatest nineteenth century novelists. Consider, for instance, the appallingly clumsy switch from first- to third-person narrative in *The Old Curiosity Shop* or the welding together of narrative strands in *Middlemarch*. In identifying 'the incoherence of the narrative line' in Lytton's *The Last Days of Pompeii*, however, Sutherland states that such infelicities are not so much 'reprehensible' as a product of the time in which the novel was written. The same can certainly be said of Lever's solecisms. There was an intense temptation to embark on new projects before the one already in hand was completed and little or no time at all was left to revise and refine. It is the high incidence of such plotless and undisciplined fictions, emanating from both sides of the Irish Sea during the first half of the nineteenth century, that weakens Anthony Cronin's contention that these features were in some way peculiarly Irish; that some Irish novelists 'may have been simply incapable of constructing an ordinary machinery of dramatic causation. It may be that some of them, like Joyce, were uninterested in doing so'.[53] Tempting though it is to suggest that the characteristics of Lever's early fiction are symptomatic of his Irishness, the theory demands an unacceptable insularity of criticism. Much more credible, and with a particular relevance to the defence of Lever as an Irishman writing for an English audience, is James M. Cahalan's examination of these common features in a specifically Irish context:

Irish novelists did not write carefully plotted novels that drew on the relationships between and among the upper, middle, and lower classes, and aimed at a largely middle class readership in their own country. Instead they more often introduced a storyteller as narrator who could only lament what was in class terms as well as in other terms a 'broken world,' as Sean O'Faolain called it, for whichever readers would 'listen,' and in the early nineteenth century those readers tended to be much more frequently English than Irish.[54]

In fact, in some ways, Lever turned this convention on its head as the world which he portrayed became more determinedly 'broken' as the discipline of his fiction increased.

He did indeed attempt to improve his methods of composition and he grew as a stylist. In speaking of Lever, Trollope stated:

What was his manner of working I do not know, but I should think it must have been very quick, and that he never troubled himself on the subject, except when he was seated with a pen in his hand.[55]

The early novels – to which Trollope referred – offer us very little evidence with which to challenge the accuracy of this impression; however, in the novels of his middle and late periods, we might detect that Lever, in the words of the *Dictionary of National Biography*, 'awoke in some measure to the claims of art'. The same source dates this 'awakening' to the composition of *Roland Cashel* (1850), but there are clear signs of a more thoughtful consideration of character and subject as early even as *Tom Burke of Ours* (1844). The shrewd and convincing characterisation of *The O'Donoghue* precludes the acceptance of any claim that his composition continued to be the product of unabated spontaneity. Even though he seemed uncertain how to end this novel – whether 'amid the lightning and thunder which scattered the French fleet in Bantry Bay'[56] or 'in Colburn and Bentley fashion, with love and marriage licences'[57] – there is a consistency of tone and an overall coherency lacking in the immature fiction. Writing to his friend Alexander Spencer of *The Knight of Gwynne* in January 1846, he declared:

I am emboldened to hope that I am improving as a writer. One thing I can answer for, – no popularity I ever had, or shall have, will make me trifle with the public by fast writing and careless composition.[58]

The failure of this novel, continuing monetary pressures, incipient physical debilitation and a growing contempt for a public which refused to acknowledge the superiority of his mature fiction, however, did not prevent him from stating, eleven years later in the preface to *The Fortunes of Glencore* (1857), that:

All I have attempted – all I have striven to accomplish – is the faithful portraiture of character, the close analysis of motives, and correct observation as to some of the manners and modes of thought which mark the age we live in.[59]

A long way, surely, from the light-hearted ease with which the incidents of *Harry Lorrequer* were 'carelessly thrown together'[60], and a forerunner of the increasingly meticulous plotting of later works such as *The Bramleighs of Bishop's Folly* in which the influence of Wilkie Collins's complex detective fiction can be identified.

– V –

Having attempted to trace the reasons behind Lever's exclusion from the popular canon of Irish literature in English, and from that of English literature, both in his own time and later, why should any effort be made to reintroduce him to a wide readership? There is, after all, no shortage of

Introduction – Writing on the Margins

nineteenth century authors available to the modern reader, and between them they might appear to cover a wide and varied range of subjects. What can Charles Lever offer that George Eliot, Dickens, Trollope or Thackeray between them cannot?

The answer, of course, is a view of the Victorian world from a peculiarly Anglo-Irish perspective. There is no other author of the mid-nineteenth century who captures so accurately and so comprehensively the anxieties, the beliefs and the prejudices of this element of society. As we have seen, in marginalising this voice – Protestant and non-separatist in tone – the rural nationalism of Daniel Corkery and his followers became allied with the Anglo-centric audience to whom Lever was accused of peddling his wares, an audience which had rejected him because of his insistence upon Irish subject matter and his criticism of English misrule. Perhaps the only Anglo-Irish contemporary of Lever's who has enjoyed anything of a renaissance is Sheridan Le Fanu, but Le Fanu, despite similar antecedents, was a writer with concerns and interests very different from those of Lever and the revival of interest in his work is centred on his novels and short stories of the supernatural. Although his early works have Irish subject matter, Le Fanu, unlike Lever, submitted to the prejudices of his English audience and abandoned Irish stories when they became unfashionable. Currently, the only other mid-nineteenth century Irish writer to enjoy any popularity is William Carleton, but Carleton's nationalism and peasant origins render him wholly acceptable to the still largely prevalent rural-Ireland school of criticism.

In his insistence upon a style of writing which incorporated strong political elements, while at the same time aiming at a large and predominantly English audience, Lever was almost unique. In seeking to entertain he also insisted upon being didactic – intending to enlighten his readers as to the nature of Ireland and to the mistakes and prejudices of its English rulers. Beginning his writing career with the desire to subsidise an extravagant mode of life he made little attempt to be either critical or analytical, but within a remarkably short period he revealed a willingness to jeopardise high earnings by refusing to curb his increasingly serious and challenging exploration of Irish society and history. The discomfort felt by many of his early readers at this marked change in direction was shared by the author himself. There is in Lever's writing a refusal to deal in platitudes and simplifications for the ease of either his audience or himself. Nowhere is this more apparent than in his treatment of the Ascendancy squirearchy, a social grouping with which he has been traditionally identified. A joyous and whole-hearted sympathy with their irresponsible high-living had, by the end of his career, converted to an unyielding condemnation of their effete and suicidal self-indulgence – this in spite of the fact that Lever saw them as the most representative symbol of the Irish Toryism which he supported. This conflict, between reason and upbringing, was a painful one for Lever – and one which he never resolved. Perhaps its most poignant expression is to be found in *Lord Kilgobbin* but its germ can be found elsewhere, even in relatively early works such as *The Martins of Cro' Martin*.

In his last novel, the male character who receives the least critical treatment is Daniel Donogan, the Fenian head-centre. Donogan is a representative of the wealthy land-holding class who has abandoned his inheritance to further the cause of Irish independence. Lever was never able to take the same step – indeed, he remained aggressively anti-Gladstone and anti-O'Connell – but his best novels constitute a literary reflection of the tortured conflict experienced by many Ascendancy thinkers. The pressures of serial publication and the concomitant failure to revise the completed instalments engendered many infelicities in the Victorian novel, but in Lever's case they give us the benefit of being able to study the formulation of his ideas and arguments. The reader can actually trace the author's struggle with the dictates of his own traditional political stance. Nowhere is this more obvious than in *The Martins of Cro' Martin* where the initially satirical portrait of the newly-emancipated Catholic bougeoisie is gradually replaced by a wholly sympathetic appraisal. These internal struggles which Lever fought throughout his maturity as a writer can, perhaps, in some ways be seen as representative of the attempt in Ireland as a whole to achieve an all-embracing political, religious and social compromise.

In *Charles Lever: New Evaluations*, Tony Bareham has described the practical difficulties of introducing Lever – and, indeed, any other neglected author – to a wide readership:

that idiotic spiral argument with publishers whereby one side argues that Lever cannot become popular until he is re-published, and the other reiterates pragmatically but not very helpfully that he can't be published until he has become widely read. [61]

Re-publication is not, in itself, enough. Admittedly, Lever's cause would be aided by an availability of texts, but it is understandable that few publishers would feel willing to invest in producing such texts without a guaranteed demand. Such a demand can only come from the schoolrooms and lecture-theatres. If Lever's novels were to be added to the syllabuses of secondary-school children and under-graduates, texts would rapidly be made available and a wider readership would naturally follow. The first battle, then, must be with those who formulate the syllabuses – most obviously, in Ireland. In recent years, the British and Irish governments have worked closely together, with the mutual goal of reaching a lasting peace-settlement in Northern Ireland. The 1998 referendum of the entire Irish population revealed an overwhelming majority in favour of accord and reconciliation (despite the continuing and bloody opposition of a minority). In fostering understanding, literature has an important part to play. This understanding must be all-embracing, it must accept – or at least recognise – schools of thought which have been excluded or marginalised. Professor R.F. Foster in his justly-acclaimed analyses of modern Irish history and of the relations between England and Ireland has examined the causes and effects of Anglo-Irish exclusion and has potently argued against its continuance. It would be difficult to find a more fitting or deserving literary symbol of conciliation and inclusion than Charles Lever.

Captain Trevanion exacts his revenge upon the insolent and murderous Frenchman, Gendemar, in *The Confessions of Harry Lorrequer* (1839). The disgust excited by this anecdote stems not only from the bestiality of the action itself but also from the cavalier, even approving manner in which Lever relates the story. In none of his more mature novels is this uncritical stance repeated.

1

THE NOVELS OF DR QUICKSILVER

– I –

Lever's reputation rests primarily upon two works of fiction: *The Confessions of Harry Lorrequer* and *Charles O'Malley – The Irish Dragoon*. These were his very first essays at authorship and, ironically, with two or three of their immediate successors, they are the least representative samples of his work. Their essential characteristics – shapelessness, boisterousness, vitality and light-heartedness – earned for him a number of sobriquets, including 'Harry Rollicker' and 'Dr Quicksilver', as well as the adulation of a significant readership on both shores of the Irish Sea. Almost overnight, they succeeded in turning an obscure physician practising medicine in Brussels into one of the best-selling authors in the English language.

In referring to his earlier novels the tone adopted by many of Lever's advocates is apologetic. The damaging criticisms first made by William Carleton[1] and later reinforced by Yeats[2] were based upon *Harry Lorrequer* and *Charles O'Malley*, upon their treatment of the Irish peasantry and upon their author's choice of Ascendancy – aristocratic and land-holding – heroes. That these criticisms had some justification is undeniable – though in refusing to acknowledge Lever's later development Yeats was guilty of, at best, ignorance, and, at worst, critical prejudice. In recognising the flaws of the early novels, many critics in their defensiveness have preferred to ascribe them to an ignoble novitiate and to rapidly pass them over, rather than to examine them in any detail or, indeed, to identify their merits. A marked exception to this rule is James M. Cahalan who, in his important though frustratingly brief analysis of Lever's work, states:

Among the few recent critical attempts to do justice to Lever's later, more serious novels, there continues a tendency to discount his earlier, light-hearted ones. In the midst of the pervasive didacticism of the nineteenth-century Irish novel ... Lever's early books are a comic breath of fresh air.[3]

This is an assessment very much at variance with Carleton's vitriolic review, in which he pilloried Lever's 'disgusting and debasing caricatures of Irish life'.

– II –

What then were the origins of *Harry Lorrequer* and what the foundations for such diametrically opposed critical view-points? In his 1872 preface to the novel, Lever gives an ingenuous account of his arbitrary manner of composition and of the very limited hopes which he entertained for his attempts at authorship:

That some thirty years after the sketches which form this volume were written I should be called on to revise and re-edit them is strange enough to me; well remembering, as I do, with what little hope of permanence they were penned, how lightly they were undertaken, and how carelessly thrown together.[4]

Originally written as a series of stories linked by very little beyond the character of their narrator, *Harry Lorrequer* was contributed to the *Dublin University Magazine* between 1837 and 1840, and in the note which accompanied his first submission, Lever made it quite clear that he had no intentions of writing a novel and that he was 'not in the vein for anything longer or more continuous than magazine work'.[5] In fact, the sketches introduced in this off-hand manner were to prove the making of the magazine, though the popularity of the series was not immediately made known to its originator who for a time remained satisfied with his seven guineas a sheet.

The foundations for the negative critical treatment of *Harry Lorrequer* and the other early novels are acutely summarised by Barry Sloan:

here the reader had a series of adventures that provoked laughter, confirmed foreign prejudices about the quaintness of the Irish peasantry, and challenged little or nothing of the complacency of mid-Victorian England in its policies towards Ireland. Quite consciously, he appealed to the literary tastes of his foreign readers in a way and to an extent greater than that of his contemporaries.[6]

Certainly Lever was writing for a readership identical with that which applauded the early works of Charles Dickens, a readership which saw him 'merely as the humorsome delineator of the rollicking, mule-cart-topping, bullet-proof dragoon'.[7] With this essentially English, middle-class and suburban audience he achieved a success unparalleled by any other Irish writer of his generation. But we might take issue with the claim that in his depiction of the peasantry Lever was guilty of a cynical exploitation deliberately tuned to the prejudices of an English readership. Admittedly, he does not offer us any profound and acutely observed portrait of the Irish peasant; in fact, he was interested very little in the labouring classes as a subject for his fiction. His personal knowledge of the peasantry was limited, far too limited, indeed, to attempt anything like the detailed and properly informed portraiture of a class with which he had little contact. This lack of knowledge made him equally ill-equipped to utilise the peasantry for overtly comic purposes. It would be going too far to suggest that he was exhibiting any particular integrity and intelligence as a writer in his decision not to attempt such a depiction, after all such inactivity could do nothing to dispel the prevalent misconceptions concerning the peasantry, but it is true that his decision prevented him from committing some of the gaucheries of his contemporary, Samuel Lover. Where Lever does deal in any detail with a peasant character, such as Mickey Free in *Charles O'Malley*, the portrait is not intended to epitomise the whole of the peasant class but rather a body of shrewd, cunning and humorous individuals within that class. Overall, it is vital to our appreciation of Lever that we accept that his *milieu* is not that of the peasant. The realism of his writings is due to his primarily concerning himself, throughout his career, with the sections of society – both Irish and international – with which he was most intimately familiar. Characters from the peasantry would feature, sometimes quite largely, in a number of his novels – *St Patrick's Eve*, for instance – but Lever's heroes and heroines are almost exclusively taken from the upper-middle and land-holding classes.

The modern-day reader of *Harry Lorrequer* does not remember the novel for the few episodes in which peasants appear, but for the sequence of ludicrous drinking, duelling and love-making adventures which befall the upper-class hero himself:

as in the later *Irish R.M.* stories of Somerville and Ross, Lever's novels exemplify the Ascendancy laughing at itself instead of at the peasantry and, rather than perpetuating the stage-Irishman, they create instead a 'stage Anglo-Irishman'.[8]

The 1872 prefaces written while Lever was British Consul in Trieste are important both for shedding light on the origins of his novels and in providing us with the author's mature opinions concerning them. The preface to *Harry Lorrequer* is no exception and in it Lever identifies himself with his first fictional hero:

To give what consistency I might to a mass of incongruous adventure, to such a variety of strange situations befalling one individual, I was obliged to imagine a character, which probably my experiences ... assured me as being perfectly possible; one of a strong will and a certain energy, rarely persistent in purpose and perpetually the sport of accident, with a hearty enjoyment of the pleasure of the hour, and a very reckless indifference to the price to be paid for it. If I looked out on my acquaintances, I believed I saw many of the traits I was bent on depicting, and for others I am half afraid I had only to take a peep into myself.[9]

It is this hero then, this peculiar amalgam of characteristics, some authorial, some observed in friends and others dictated by the demands of the fiction's coherency, who rides a whirligig of comical adventures that hurtles across Ireland and the Continent, eventually concluding in Munich.

Where *Harry Lorrequer* may be at variance with the expectations of the modern audience is in the apparent lack of distance between the attitudes of its hero and those of the author. This lack of distance lends substance to Edmund Downey's statement that the novel is written from 'points of view which indicate some obliquity or narrowness of vision'.[10] In his chaotic career Lorrequer passes from duel to duel and from one romantic dalliance to the next, hardly ever pausing to draw breath. In chapter eleven, for instance, having discovered the supposed treachery of Lady Jane Callonby – Lorrequer's 'true love' and the closest approximation to a heroine in this male-dominated fiction – the hero gives brief consideration to his eventful history:

I had drawn my chair to the corner of the ample fireplace, and in a half-dreamy state was reviewing the incidents of my early life, and like most men who, however young, have still to lament talents misapplied, opportunities neglected, profitless labour, and disastrous idleness.[11]

But within a very few moments he is caught up in an audacious plot to woo and elope with Mary, daughter of the veteran Colonel Kamworth and heiress to two-hundred thousand pounds! The blow inflicted by Jane Callonby's desertion is viewed almost wholly in terms of its detrimental effects on Lorrequer's reputation with his peers, the wound to his sensibilities hardly entering into the equation:

although much and warmly attached to Lady Jane Callonby, and feeling most acutely what I must call her abandonment of me, yet, the most constantly recurring idea of my mind on the subject was, what will the mess say? – what will they think at head-quarters? – the raillery, the jesting, the half-concealed allusion, the tone of assumed compassion, which all awaited me, as each of my companions took up his line of behaving towards me, was, after all, the most difficult thing to be borne.[12]

In a character exhibiting such susceptibilities any attempt at moralising seems but a momentary aberration. Furthermore, in the relation of such incidents as the confrontation between Captain Trevanion and the pugnacious Frenchman Capitaine Gendemar, the narrator's tone is one of admiration for the English officer:

> Le Capitaine ... with a nod of most insulting familiarity, saluted Trevanion, adding with a loud voice, so as to be heard on every side – 'A votre courage, Anglais.' He had scarcely swallowed the liquor, when Trevanion rose slowly from his chair, displaying to the astonished Frenchman the immense proportions and gigantic frame of a man well-known as the largest man in the British army; with one stride he was beside the chair of the Frenchman, and with the speed of lightning he seized his nose by one hand, while with the other he grasped his lower jaw, and, wrenching open his mouth with the strength of an ogre, he spat down his throat.[13]

Throughout this scene, and the introduction to it, there is not a trace of irony. Rather, Trevanion's action – which produces absolute revulsion in the modern reader – appears to excite the author's whole-hearted approbation. Within the novel Lorrequer and his fellow protagonists seem to operate in what can only be described as a moral vacuum: actions which a modern audience might view variously as callous, blood-thirsty, or actually bestial, are committed without a trace of authorial criticism, whether explicit or implied. A dark counterpart, perhaps, of what Anthony Cronin has identified as the 'curious stancelessness' of Maria Edgeworth's *Castle Rackrent*.

To counter-balance such criticisms it can be argued that in *Harry Lorrequer* we find a quite convincing depiction of youth, in its light-hearted indifference to the possible repercussions of one's actions. It is this comic, youthful boisterousness which won for Lever the hearts of his readership, and this characteristic remains the novel's greatest individual merit. The break-neck pace of the narrative is established within the very first pages, which describe the 'civic festivities' in Cork:

> When I first returned to consciousness, I found myself lying exactly where I had fallen. Around me lay heaps of slain ... The room we were in was a small one off the great saloon, and through the half-open folding-door I could clearly perceive that the festivities were still continued. The crash of fiddles and French horns, and the tramp of feet, which had lost much of their elasticity since the entertainment began, rang through my ears, mingled with the sounds of 'Down the middle', 'Hands across', 'Here's your partner, captain'. What hour of the night or morning it then was, I could not guess; but certainly the vigour of the party seemed little abated, if I might judge from the specimen before me, and the testament of a short plethoric gentleman, who stood wiping his bald head, after conducting his partner down twenty-eight couple, and who, turning to his friend, said, 'Oh, the distance is nothing, but it is the pace that kills.'[14]

This passage is representative of much that follows, but the reader's interest never flags; there is enough of variety and drollery to sustain Lever not only through *Harry Lorrequer* but through a handful of novels. Indeed, he was later to admit that at this time he thought his reservoir of high-spirits to be unfathomable.

Always remembering the artless nature of its composition, Lever never attempted to endow *Harry Lorrequer* with a *gravitas* which the novel could not sustain, but James M. Cahalan has recently suggested that the undisciplined nature of the early fiction is symptomatic of the long tradition of oral story-telling in Ireland:

> Why do Irish novels tend to have strong narrators and weak plots? Perhaps partly because of the power and longevity of the oral storytelling tradition in Ireland, as well as the virtual absence of a middle class in Ireland as both subject and audience. These two crucial features of Irish society led the Irish novel in its form far away from English novels.[15]

Whether we choose to attack this insubstantial and rambling work with all the weapons of modern politico-critical authority, or to defend its seemingly directionless narrative as a natural extension of an ancient tradition, the novel's main function is as a yard-stick by which to measure a number of later works, particularly through contrasting its endless jollity with the dourness which marks the fiction of Lever's maturity. The gleeful depictions of the debauchery of both provincial and vice-regal society in the early works are later replaced by biting and satirical authorial condemnation. Furthermore, the mature novels altogether eschew the political carelessness objected to by Barry Sloan:

> The problems of Ireland and the Irish people which so preoccupied the earlier Anglo-Irish novelists cause Lever's conscience little trouble in his first books ... Nevertheless, by the end of the novel, the hero is set to assume responsibility as Under Secretary for Ireland![16]

By the time of writing *Lord Kilgobbin* Lever could refer to the appointment of such political *ingenues* with a bitter sarcasm bearing little resemblance to his early off-handedness. Moreover, the novel's cavalier treatment of women – who in *Harry Lorrequer* seldom develop beyond the condition of mere ciphers and routes for masculine advancement – is also rapidly replaced by a shrewd and sympathetic examination of their plight and, indeed, a heartfelt plea for the improvement of their condition. Most important of all, however, is the almost instantaneous development of a moral conscience. Never again would Lever's heroes or heroines act without their actions being accompanied by a critical authorial analysis which was already beginning to find expression when his second novel was composed.

– III –

Charles O'Malley offers a far more rewarding field of study than *Harry Lorrequer*, despite Lever's avowal of his unreformed method of composition:

> When, therefore, my publishers asked me could I write a story in the *Lorrequer* vein . . . I was ready to reply – Not one, but fifty. Do not mistake me, and suppose that any overweening confidence in my literary powers would have emboldened me to make this reply; my whole strength lay in the fact that I could not recognise anything like literary effort in the matter. If the world would only condescend to read that which I wrote precisely as I was in the habit of talking, nothing could be easier than for me to occupy them.[17]

While there is the same rambling, anecdotal narrative progression, revealing little of the art of careful plotting, greater literary effort can be identified in the pages of this novel. Lever himself acknowledged that, 'I was in a measure training myself for what, without my then knowing it, was to become my career in life'.[18]

He continues to revel in the riotous, and indeed ruinous, high-living of the Irish landowning classes, and in doing so produces some of the funniest episodes penned by an Irishman in any century. In discussing the early Trinity College scenes, James M. Cahalan recognises that Lever's decision to write a novel with a comic rather than a deliberately political or historical purpose, in no way impinges upon the work's value or, indeed, upon its 'Irishness'.[19] He also links Lever's name with those of Flann O'Brien and J.P. Donleavy, thereby placing him very firmly in the company of the greatest literary exponents of Irish humour, and this whilst analysing one of the novels which has been the foundation of Lever's ostracism from the ranks of Ireland's established canon of respected writers! The comic exuberance and irreverence of *Charles O'Malley* might be represented by an incident in chapter sixteen, in which the parsimonious and blasphemous Vice-provost is bated by Mickey Free, O'Malley's servant and a character who, according to Fitzpatrick, 'attained a celebrity second only to Sam Weller':[20]

> Boring a hole in a halfpenny, he attached a long string to it, and, having dropped it on the Doctor's step, stationed himself on the opposite side of the court . . . He waited patiently for the chapel bell, at the first toll of which the Doctor issued forth. Scarcely was his foot upon the step, when he saw the piece of money, and as quickly stooped to seize it; but just as his finger had nearly touched it, it evaded his grasp, and slowly retreated. He tried again but with the like success. At last, thinking he miscalculated the distance, he knelt leisurely down, and put forth his hand; but lo! it again escaped him; on which, slowly rising from his posture, he shambled on towards the chapel, where meeting the senior lecturer at the door, he cried out, 'H— to my soul, Wall, but I saw the halfpenny walk away!'[21]

Traditionally, many of the comic Trinity incidents are believed to have been based upon Lever's own college career. One such attribution is the episode in which O'Malley's room-mate, Frank Webber, persuades a crowd in Grafton Street to dig up the drains in an attempt to liberate an escaped felon who has become lost in its labyrinthine passages. A scene which has been described as 'an episode of sheer absurdity as well as a bizarre commentary on the power of Irish patriotism':[22]

'Where did he come from?' 'Who is he?' 'How did he get there?' were questions on every side, and various surmises were afloat, till Webber, rising from his knees, said, in a mysterious whisper to those nearest him, 'He's made his escape to-night out o' Newgate by the big drain, and lost his way; he was looking for the Liffey, and took the wrong turn.'

To an Irish mob, what appeal could equal this? A culprit, at any time, has his claim upon their sympathy; but let him be caught in the very act of cheating the authorities and evading the law, and his popularity knows no bounds. Webber knew this well, and as the mob thickened around him, sustained an imaginary conversation that Savage Landor might have envied, imparting now and then such hints concerning the runaway as raised their interest to the highest pitch.[23]

The brilliance of the narration is undeniable, but its absolute originality might, perhaps, be questioned. An almost totally forgotten English novelist, Henry Cockton, had, prior to the commencement of *Charles O'Malley*, begun the serialisation of his novel *Valentine Vox the Ventriloquist*. In chapter thirteen of this obscure work there is an episode in which the eponymous hero uses his voice-throwing gifts to convince the visitors and staff of the British Museum that a labourer – coincidentally, an Irish labourer – has become trapped in an Egyptian sarcophagus:

The lid happened to be down, and as it was obvious that Mr Jones had entered the Museum expressly in order to be astonished, it occurred to Valentine that it would be a pity to allow him to depart disappointed. He therefore, while apparently admiring with others an exceedingly broad Egyptian pedestal, introduced a quiet groan into the sepulchre, as Jones was engaged in pointing out to his friend the ridiculous character of certain hieroglyphics.

'Hush! hush!' cried that gentleman, starting back suddenly and seizing the arm of his friend. Hush! didn't you hear?'

'I thought I heard something,' observed his friend, whispering.

'Hush! hush-sh! Listen!' and Valentine sent in another small groan.

'Send I may live! – 'tis a man!' exclaimed Jones.

'Impossible!' cried his friend. 'Why, do you know the age of this thing?'

'I don't care a dump about the age! If it is in its fifty millionth year it don't matter a button: there's something alive in it now – listen again!' and the violence of his action drew several persons round, anxious to ascertain what had caused so much excitement.[24]

In a manner almost identical with the rescue attempts in *Charles O'Malley* there is a desperate and comical bid to release the unfortunate before he expires through lack of air. The similarities in the two episodes are, indeed, so pronounced that one must wonder whether the Grafton Street hoax was suggested by the slightly earlier invention of an otherwise inferior writer.

– IV –

Although *Charles O'Malley* remains remarkable for the quality and exuberance of its comedy, the novel also reveals a marked increase of seriousness in many episodes. There is a definite augmentation of the dramatic incidents which results in a variation of pace and tone far superior to the unremitting boisterousness of *Harry Lorrequer*. Such scenes begin early and continue to punctuate the novel's entirety at varying intervals. One of the first incidents of this nature is the duel between O'Malley and Bodkin in chapter eight, in which the narrative tone is very different from that used to describe a similar event in *Harry Lorrequer*. In the earlier novel the hero proceeds to the duelling ground with a light-heartedness typical of the whole book but, to the modern reader at least, ill-according with the blood-thirsty nature of the meeting:

'Truly,' thought I, 'there is no equanimity like his who acts as your second in a duel. The gentlemanlike urbanity with which he waits on the opposite friend – the conciliating tone with which he proffers implacable enmity – the killing kindness with which he refuses all accommodation – the Talleyrand air of his short notes . . . all indicative of the friendly precipitancy of the negotiation . . .'[25]

By contrast, the preface to the duel in *Charles O'Malley* reveals a narrator rapidly maturing both in skill and in sensibility. The wording is comparatively terse and there is no clumsy attempt at philosophy; instead the drama is provided largely through the use of dialogue, the authorial attitude is implied rather than given explicit expression and the flippancy of Bodkin's duelling recollections is deliberately intended to arouse the reader's disgust:

'Poor devil,' said Bodkin, 'it wasn't his fault . . . Well, out he came: it was a cold morning in February, with a frost the night before going off in a thin rain: well, it seems he had the consumption or something of that sort, with a great cough and spitting of blood, and this weather made him worse, and he was very weak when he came to the ground. Now, the moment I got a glimpse of him, I said to myself, "He's pluck enough, but as nervous as a lady;" for his eyes wandered all about, and his mouth was constantly twitching. "Take off your greatcoat, Ned," said one of his people, when they were going to put him up; "take it off, man." He seemed to hesitate for an instant, when Michael Blake remarked, "Arrah, let him alone; it's his mother makes him wear it, for the cold he has." They all began to laugh at this, but I kept my eye upon him. And I saw that his cheek grew quite livid, and a kind of grey colour, and his eyes filled up. "I have you now," said I to myself, and I shot him through the lungs.'[26]

The raconteur's tone is not at all dissimilar to that of Lorrequer, but the details of the victim – his consumption and his nervousness – and of the nature of the injury inflicted, produce a very different reaction from that intended in the first novel. The two chapters in question also develop in a manner entirely unlike: while Lorrequer proceeds to further drunken revelry in the house of Father Malachi, O'Malley is forced to flee for his life, pursued by the vengeful tenants of his wounded opponent. Lever's treatment of duelling would continue to develop throughout his career, to the point in *Sir Brook Fossbrooke* where the *denouement* of the novel's somewhat melodramatic plot is provided not by an exchange of shots and the villain's timely demise, but rather by a duel's failure to take place at all.

Perhaps the most dramatic episode in *Charles O'Malley* occurs in chapter forty-four, when the hero returns from the Peninsula Campaigns. As Tony Bareham has shown,[27] it is at this point in the novel that Lever successfully creates a 'false ending' apparently retiring his hero from the army shortly before the most important battle of any European war in the nineteenth century. Of course, O'Malley again volunteers and sees action at Waterloo, but it is in the scenes climaxing with the false ending that we find some of the greatest drama in the novel. Having been informed of his uncle's serious illness, the hero rushes homewards, and, almost within sight of O'Malley Castle pauses to rest and to collect his thoughts:

Overcome for the instant by my exertion and my emotion, I sat down upon the stone, and, taking off my cap, bathed my heated and throbbing temples in the cold spring. Refreshed at once, I was about to rise and press onward, when suddenly my attention was caught by a sound which, faint from distance, scarce struck upon my ear. I listened again, but all was still and silent, the dull plash of the river, as it broke upon the reedy shore, was the only sound I heard. Thinking it probably some mere delusion of my heated imagination, I rose to push forward; but at that moment a slight breeze stirred in the leaves around me, the light branches rustled and bent beneath it, and a low, moaning sound swelled upwards, increasing each instant as it came: like the distant roar of some mighty torrent it grew louder as the wind bore it towards me, and now falling, now swelling, it burst forth into one loud prolonged cry of agony and grief.[28]

What O'Malley hears is the grief-stricken keen of his uncle's mourners, but the desolation of the setting and the ebb and flux of the sound itself lend the description the quality of the supernatural. In a translation not unworthy of the early century's gothic romances, the sound created by the mourners' emotion becomes redolent of the banshee's haunting and doom-laden cry.

– V –

As Lionel Stevenson points out,[29] *Harry Lorrequer* 'had been a military novel only in the sense that its hero was an officer', and actual warfare plays no part in the narrative. *Charles O'Malley*, however, was 'military in its very inception' and much of the novel takes place in the thick of the Peninsula Campaigns. In his 1872 preface Lever acknowledged the increased difficulties which describing well-recorded events entailed:

> I can recall, too, and I am afraid more vividly still, some of the difficulties of my task when I endeavoured to form anything like an accurate or precise idea of some campaigning incident, or some passage of arms, from the narratives of two distinct and separate 'eye-witnesses'. What mistrust I conceived for all eye-witnesses from my own brief experience of their testimonies![30]

The new novel was clearly an undertaking which made far heavier demands upon its author, but in encountering these increased difficulties, he achieved considerable success. Although he never saw military service himself, Lever's depictions of battle have an immediacy which discounts any possibility of their being mere reworkings of text-book descriptions, and yet artistic licence was not allowed to weigh heavier in the balance than accuracy. In combining details from standard authorities with the eye-witness accounts of his military acquaintances in Brussels, he was able to create scenes which, whilst having enough of excitement and vitality to keep his readers rapt also convinced many actual combatants that the author must be of their number.[31]

In analysing the writings of Sir Walter Scott and James Fennimore Cooper, Honore de Balzac stated that the most successful military fiction is that which concerns itself with the intimate experience of battle:

> They never attempted a campaign in their works, but confined themselves to small encounters, revealing through them the spirit of the two contending masses. And even these small skirmishes which they undertook required lengthy preparation in their works.[32]

Lever does make some attempt to outline the progress of the Peninsula Campaigns and, in the closing chapters of *Charles O'Malley*, from his vantage point as a prisoner of the French, the eponymous hero describes the panorama of the Battle of Waterloo. It is not these moments of broad spectacle which produce the greatest impact on the reader, however, but those which capture the immediacy of battle, as felt by the individual combatants. In the pages of *Charles O'Malley* we find some of the most powerful fictional descriptions of battle penned in the nineteenth century. Lever brings to his reader's nostrils the very whiff of gunpowder:

> the word 'March' passed in whispers from rank to rank, and the dark mass moved on. What a moment was that, as we advanced to the foot of the breach! The consciousness that at the same instant, from different points of that vast plain, similar parties were moving on; the feeling that, at a word, the flame of the artillery and the flash of steel would spring from that dense crowd, and death and carnage in every shape our imagination can conceive be dealt on all sides! . . .
> A deafening roll of musketry from the extreme right announced that the Third Division was already in action, while the loud cry of our leader as he sprang into the trench summoned us to the charge . . . A loud rumbling thunder crept along the earth, a hissing, crackling noise followed, and from the dark ditch a forked and livid lightning burst like the flame from a volcano, and a mine exploded . . . the whole fortress seemed girt around with fire.[33]

To verify the accuracy of this account one need only compare it with the descriptions of the mines ignited under the German lines during the First World War, for instance at the Battle of Messines in June 1917 – over seventy years after he was writing:

> The waiting infantry felt the shocks and heard the rumble of an earthquake. It seemed as if the Messines Ridge got up and shook itself. All along its flank belched rows of mushroom-shaped masses of debris, flung high into the air.[34]

Taking the raw material accumulated during innumerable convivial gatherings, Lever, with consummate artistry moulded a breath-taking narrative of military endeavour, which is far more than a mere recitation of after-dinner anecdotes, or a blow-by-blow rendition of tactics and strategy.

Ironically, as an author he may have benefitted from his lack of military experience, from his having never witnessed the devastation of armed conflict. Through not having to contend with a personal familiarity with bloodshed, he was perhaps able to dwell on scenes and events which had, for him, none of the horror of actuality. In their depictions of battle, some soldiers-turned-authors, such as the now neglected George Whyte-Melville and Lever's mentor William Hamilton Maxwell, resort to an objectivity which undoubtedly detracts from the power of their narratives. In *The Fortunes of Hector O'Halloran* (1843) Maxwell's descriptions of the Peninsula Campaigns – in which he had participated – are actually reminiscent of a text-book analysis; whilst Whyte-Melville, despite a very real talent, in his novel *The Interpreter* (1858), makes very little use of his Crimean experiences and instead involves himself in the intricacies of a convoluted romantic plot. Lever, in his imaginative portrayal of warfare might better be compared with the American novelist, Steven Crane, whose *Red Badge of Courage* (1895) describes the confusion and fear of the American Civil War. While we cannot claim for Lever, at this stage in his career, the psychological insight revealed in Crane's most famous work, *Charles O'Malley* is far more than a romanticised view of war as a boyish adventure. There are a number of scenes in the novel where the camaraderie of soldierly life and the military 'virtues' of heroism and excitement give way to the darker experiences of the battlefield, O'Malley's survey of the carnage of Waterloo, for instance:

As my eye ranged over this harrowing spectacle, a dreadful anxiety shot through me as I asked myself whose had been the victory. A certain confused impression of flight and pursuit remained in my mind: but, at the moment, the circumstances of my own position in the early part of the day increased the difficulty of reflection, and left me in a state of intense and agonising uncertainty. [35]

In his inability to ascertain who has achieved victory, in his emotions when viewing the casualties of the conflict, and in his mention of 'those vultures of the battlefield who strip alike the dead and dying', Lever's account becomes a grim presage of the realism of Crane's narrative.

– VI –

In reviewing *Charles O'Malley*, Lever's earlier biographers dwell on its characterisation – rightly so, since the novel contains some of his finest comic creations. That he drew heavily upon the quirks of his friends we know well; indeed, Thackeray's daughter, Lady Ritchie, would later recall her father's conversational reference to 'Lever who puts all his acquaintances into his books'.[36] Incidentally, this was not a trait which Lever appreciated in other writers. In Florence he studiously avoided the company of Frances Trollope, for fear that she would choose him to feature in one of her own fictions – an unsuccessful tactic apparently, since scenes in her novel *The Old World and the New* (c1846), were almost certainly based on his life.

Lever willingly admitted his penchant for borrowing from life and saw no reason to apologise for it:

The principle of natural selection adapts itself to novels as to nature, and it would have demanded an effort above my strength to have disabused myself at the desk of all the impressions of the dinner-table, and to have forgotten features which interested or amused me.[37]

Indeed, in the 1872 preface to *Charles O'Malley* he gives a lengthy account of his acquaintance with Commissary-General Mayne, the original of the morally-ambiguous Major Monsoon. The identity of other sources of inspiration were easily recognised by their contemporaries, and in at least one instance Lever actually forgot to grace his portrait with a fictitious name!

In his depiction of the wild life of the impecunious Galway gentry and of the bivouac Lever is unsurpassed, but there is one particular character to whom, above all others, critical attention should be directed: Mickey Free. It is to Mickey that Lever's critics point when accusing him of pandering to foreign prejudices concerning the Irish peasant. In fact, though deliberately comical, Mickey is no mere clown or buffoon; the portrait is humorous but not derisory, and a fair comparison might be made with Dickens's creation, Samuel Weller – a character to whom few Cockneys would seriously object. As Lever admitted, Mickey was not a fictionalised depiction of one individual, as in the cases of Major Monsoon or the delightful Baby Blake, but an amalgam of 'one thousand types'.[38] On his introduction to the reader Mickey is painted in glowing colours:

> he was possessed of a very great flow of gossiping conversation. He knew all that was doing in the country, and never was barren in his information wherever his imagination could come into play. Mickey was the best hurler in the barony, no mean performer on the violin, could dance the national bolero of 'Tatter Jack Walsh' in a way that charmed more than one soft heart beneath a red wolsey bodice, and had, withal, the peculiar free-and-easy devil-may-care kind of off-hand Irish way that never deserted him in the midst of his wiliest and most subtle moments, giving to a very deep and cunning fellow all the apparent frankness and openness of a country lad.[39]

Mickey's physical prowess is more than matched by his quick intelligence and these qualities stay with him throughout the novel. While some of the funniest moments in the entire narrative – such as his bating the Vice-provost of Trinity, or his claim to have sung duets with Wellington – are attributable to Mickey's drollery and high spirits, at no time is he shown to be anybody's fool, rather he is able to play on the gullibility of others. In a scene that would not be out of place in Kipling's works, for instance, we find him surrounded by battle-hardened veterans who willingly perform his chores in return for samples of his irrepressible pleasantry:

> Mr Free was, as described, most leisurely reposing on a bank, a mug of something drinkable beside him ... He appeared to be giving his directions to some soldiers of the troop, who were busily cleaning his horses and accoutrements for him.
>
> 'That's it, Jim! Rub 'em down along the jocks. He won't kick; it's only play.

Scrub away, honey; that's the devil's own carbine to get clean.'
'Well, I say, Mr Free, are you going to give us that 'ere song?'
'Yes; I'll be danged if I burnish your sabre if you don't sing.'
'Tear an' ages! ain't I composin' it? Av I was Tommy Moore I couldn't be quicker.'[40]

In essence, Mickey's traits are all good ones, and the reader is generally invited to laugh with, rather than at him. The negative features of the characterisation are, indeed, those which have been grafted onto the portrait by a later unforgiving and Nationalist criticism:

This class of criticism is born either of ignorance or of jealousy or of crassness ... Of Irish peasant life he did not possess that intimate knowledge – it can be acquired only through actual experience – that Carleton possessed; but in none of Lever's books is there to be found anything bordering on disgusting and debasing caricatures of the peasantry.[41]

The use of phonetic spelling to indicate the peasant idiom remains irritating to the modern ear, but in his use of such a device Lever was rather following the example of his contemporaries than creating an original means of linguistic portrayal. Should we continue to react so violently to what is really, at worst, an unsuccessful attempt to replicate peasant speech patterns, when Dickens's equally clumsy Vs for Ws Cockney-English raises not so much as an eyebrow? Very soon Lever would abandon the device and relieve his peasant characters of this forced and unnecessary comicality. Mickey Free may not be the most profound study of the Irish peasant, as it might be said that Weller is not a character who allows us to fathom fully the depths of the late Georgian lower-class urban-dweller, but the fact is that neither creation was intended to fulfil such a function. Both are intended, primarily, to entertain and both do so very effectively within their prescribed limits.

In her essay on *Charles O'Malley*, Lorna Reynolds argues that the work 'is not just a tale of knight-errantry: it is also a *bildungsroman*: a novel that depicts the education of the hero in life'.[42] And that, by the end of the narrative:

Charles has been educated, not only in heroic action, but in the affairs of the heart. He had escaped the dangers of the battlefield but also the false allurements that can beset a young man, the temptations of flirtation and of propinquity; he has remained true to the star that guides and inspires. He had to leave his home to find himself but he returns to fulfil the promise of his youth.[43]

Despite the hero's education and, indeed, the development of his creator, there remains a shallowness in O'Malley's character: his motivation remains uncomplicated and far more limited than that which spurs the later heroes. Nonetheless, Lever's skill in characterisation had taken an important leap forward. He exhibits a far deeper interest in the inner-workings of his protagonist's mind and in his relationships with the other characters – particularly in those with his uncle and with the Count Considine, an early example of the canny and sage advisors who appear in a number of the later works. In O'Malley's thoughts on his uncle's death, for instance, we find sentiments expressed which we would never expect from the irrepressible Lorrequer:

> Life had lost its charm for me; my gratified ambition had ended in the blackest disappointment, and all for which I had laboured and longed was only attained that I might feel it valueless.
> Of my circumstances as to fortune I knew nothing, and cared not more; poverty and riches could matter little now... The daily association with objects which recalled but one image to my brain, and that evermore accompanied by remorse of conscience, gave me not a moment's peace. My every thought of happiness was mixed up with scenes which now presented nothing but the evidences of blighted hope: to remain, then, where I was, would be to sink into the heartless misanthropist. [44]

O'Malley, of course, regains his spirits, but it is through such episodes that Lever succeeds in engaging the sympathies of his readers. We might enjoy the light-hearted mayhem of *Harry Lorrequer* but through the varied tone of the later work and through the hero's genuine attempts at self-examination, *Charles O'Malley* actually involves us in the action and we are propelled beyond the condition of mere spectators.

– VII –

In discussing Lever's early novels, Barry Sloan reduces them to mere 'collections of episodic adventures, anecdotes, songs and romantic encounters'.[45] Although this is a fair summary of *Harry Lorrequer*, as a work of fiction *Charles O'Malley* is far weightier than this analysis allows. In a number of significant ways it represents an important advance on the previous work and its achievements – particularly in the powerful descriptions of battle – make it far less ephemeral. Lorna Reynolds's summary is rather more just:

> *Charles O'Malley* is in essence a serious work... a young man's novel about a young man: it portrays well the idealism and charm of youth.[46]

In reading the novel we might feel justified in questioning Lever's statement that, 'I wrote as I felt; sometimes in good spirits, sometimes in bad, always carelessly, for, God help me! I can do no better'.[47] In many places, *Charles O'Malley* exhibits considerable care in its composition and a calculated engineering of various emotional effects.

To twentieth century eyes, the novel does suffer from being over-long; and even at the time of its publication in America, Edgar Allen Poe, in a severe review, complained 'in the story proper are repetitions without end'.[48] Some of the fault we might place at the door of Lever's publisher, M'Glashan, who persuaded the author, against his will to prolong the narrative:

> a project, my pocket, but not my brains, concurs in. I fear much that the public may grow very weary of the mere narrative details of battle and bloodshed... the fear is, shall I not mar all by spinning out?[49]

Unfortunately, Lever too often subordinated his artistic integrity to the demands of his publisher. However, the charge of prolixity might be levelled at many a mid-Victorian author – including not a few whose place in the established canon remains undisputed.

We know from his correspondence that – largely because of illness – Lever found the composition of *Charles O'Malley* an arduous task, and we may attribute some of the novel's faults – including his apparent inability to marshal his material – to this fact. But we also know that in embarking on his second work of fiction, he was not interested in a mere mercenary duplication of a previously successful formula:

> I am working away, *malgre* gout and dyspepsia, but by no means satisfied with my labours or sanguine about their success. So long as I had done nothing I felt indifferent on this head, but the unmerited success of *Lorrequer* has stimulated me to do better.[50]

He wanted to 'do better' and *Charles O'Malley* reveals a significant development in his approach to authorship. Certainly he created a host of brilliantly observed comic characters and used them to populate a series of wonderfully hilarious and memorable adventures. Perhaps more significantly, he created one of the finest fictional depictions of the Napoleonic campaigns. In writing of this aspect of the novel, Lionel Stevenson states:

> In those days the soldiers were professionals with no pretensions to authorship, and the novelists were stay-at-homes who lacked the opportunities for learning much about the campaigns.[51]

Lever, however, with his life-long fascination with all things military, endows his narrative with a sympathetic immediacy and though some writers 'had shown the possibilities of the theme ... Lever was the first to capitalize it'.[52] By the time of writing *Charles O'Malley* he was already well on his way to coming of age as a novelist, and a soulless duplication of the light-hearted, artless drollery of *Harry Lorrequer* was becoming increasingly unlikely.

Mark O'Donoghue dispatches the scheming land-agent Hemsworth in *The O'Donoghue* (1845). While Lever does not detail the circumstances of the rebellion of the United Irishmen, by the time of writing his sixth novel, he had travelled a considerable distance since the early works in which the actions of the central characters are seen to shape the narrative. The novel has been compared by some critics with a *Boy's Own* style adventure, but the underlying bitterness and resentment of the brooding hero belie this comparison and as the novel reaches its climax, he is swept along unable to resist the momentum of the events in which he has become embroiled.

2

A YEAR OF GROWTH

– I –

The year 1845 can be seen as a watershed in Lever's career as a novelist. Moving away from the rambling and essentially light-hearted tales which had won for him such enormous popularity, he placed before his readership two novels of an entirely different nature: *The O'Donoghue* and *St Patrick's Eve*. In these works we discover a new seriousness of intent, a fresh authorial voice and a concern with the political and social status of Ireland which would remain evident in practically everything to issue from his pen over the next twenty-seven years. These two novels and their successors belie the still prevalent belief that as an Ascendancy Irishman writing for a middle-class English audience he was unwilling to make any attempt to reform his readers' misconceptions of Ireland and the Irish.

In the first and by far the largest of these two works the plot centres on the lives and loves of two families dwelling in the south-west of Ireland in the period preceding the rebellion of 1798 and concludes with the attempted French landing in Bantry Bay in 1796. Although Lever 'treats the uprising in the most superficial way, reducing its events to a tale of misguided romantic adventure'[1] bedevilled by treachery and maladministration, he does take the opportunity to make lengthy criticisms of the English government's ineptitude and digresses to consider both the plight and the character of the Irish peasantry.

Of the two families around whom the action revolves, one is that of an Englishman, Sir Marmaduke Travers, who has come to Ireland for the first time to take stock of his newly acquired estate. Chapter fifteen of the novel is devoted to describing the failure of such English landlords to understand the nature of their tenants and to a detailed criticism of their ill-conceived plans for improvement:

Every moment disclosed some case where, in his honest efforts to improve the condition of the people, ignorance of their habits, from total unconsciousness of the social differences of two nations essentially unlike, he discovered the failure of his plans, and unhesitatingly ascribed to the prejudices of the peasantry what with more justice might have been charged against his own unskilfulness.[2]

Throughout the chapter, and indeed throughout the novel, Sir Marmaduke is seen to be a well-intentioned meddler who has no understanding of what he is attempting to alter. In contrast, his tenants are described as shrewd and practical – well able to accurately assess the character and crotchets of their landlord. Furthermore, while the tenants in their poverty look upon the Englishman with humour and compassion he, though benefiting from all the comforts and security of unassailable wealth, is all too ready to believe them 'incurably sunk in barbarism and superstition'. This disparity in attitude and understanding invariably favours the peasants and in this conflict of interests our sympathy is always engaged in the behalf of those whose good-humour is maintained in circumstances of hardship and hopelessness:

Men spoke of their light-heartedness, their gaiety of temper, their flashing and brilliant wit. How little they knew that such qualities, by some strange incongruity of our natures, are the accompaniments of deeply-reflective and imaginative minds, overshadowed by lowering fortune.[3]

Such would hardly seem to be the sentiments of a novelist often derided for his willingness to amuse his audience with cheap portrayals of the 'stage Irishman'. While the delineation of the peasantry is a purely secondary concern within the confines of the novel, it plays a vital role in our understanding of how Lever's own attitudes and his attempts to express those attitudes had developed from his earlier writings.

– II –

In *The O'Donoghue* Lever makes no attempt to trace the origins of the United Irishmen movement to its roots in radical Ulster Presbyterianism, or to examine its links with rural-based Catholic 'Defenderism'. He is, in fact, altogether very little concerned with the movement's significance as a step towards multilateral republicanism. Despite his willingness to gloss over the complexities of the rebellion, however, the structure and events of the novel do not justify Barry Sloan's statement that *The O'Donoghue* 'bears recognisable marks of Lever's earlier style with his predilection for turning everything into a rather boyish adventure with no clear scale of priorities'.[4] Indeed, it can be argued that the novel possesses a very real and quite clearly defined scale of priorities, though this may seldom coincide with Sloan's politically Nationalist criteria. It can come as no surprise to any reader of Lever's work that his scale is topped with a concern for the accurate and sympathetic portrayal of character. This novel reveals a marked development in his style in that he avoids his old propensity for humorous digression and instead concentrates on a relentless delineation of the character of Mark O'Donoghue, a hero – or, perhaps more accurately, an anti-hero – of a stamp very different from the Charles O'Malleys and Harry Lorrequers of the early fiction.

It is in the O'Donoghue family that we find the most interesting and engaging studies of the novel. Despised by the ruthless and acquisitive agent of Sir Marmaduke's estate, Captain Hemsworth, and the object of the English landlord's wry condescension, the O'Donoghues are the ancient masters of the land:

men who, with all the traditions and many of the pretensions of birth and fortune, had really become in ideas, modes of life, and habits, very little above the peasantry around them. They inhabited, it is true, the 'great house', and they were in name the owners of the soil; but, crippled by debt and overborne by mortgages, they subsisted in a shifty conflict with their creditors, rack-renting their miserable tenants to maintain it.[5]

The head of the clan is the O'Donoghue himself, a loose-living, devil-may-care country squire of the *Castle Rackrent* mould. His extravagance and bad management have completed the ruin of his family's fortune, and he has had the bad luck not only to outlive his wealth but to father two sons whose future is anything but secure. The older of the two is Mark, whose education has been limited to 'pride of family' and to the gentlemanly pursuits of hunting and riding. His trials and tribulations form the hub of the novel's action and in his detailed characteris-ation lies the book's greatest merit.

There are episodes in which Mark may seem to share the nature of the boyishly adventurous Charles O'Malley: in chapter four, for instance, in a scene reminiscent of the hunt in chapter four of the earlier novel, Mark indulges in a reckless gallop across the countryside on the horse which he has just sold to the iniquitous Lanty Lawler:

'There he goes, the jewel; see him in the stubble-field; sure it's a real picture to see him going along at his ease. Whurroo – he's over the wall. What the devil's the matter now? – they're away.' And so it was; the animal that an instant before was cantering perfectly in hand, had now set off at top speed and at full stretch. 'See the gate – mind the gate, Master Mark – tear and ages, mind the gate!' shouted Kerry, as though his admonition could be heard half a mile away. 'Oh, Holy Mary! he's through it!' And true enough – the wild and now affrighted beast dashed through the frail timbers, and held on her course without stopping. 'He's broke the gate to flitters.'[6]

Another example is to be found in chapter twenty-seven where Mark and the French agent, Talbot, stake a wager on their ability to uncork a bottle of wine using not a corkscrew but a pistol shot. Although there is in the externals of such incidents a light-hearted boisterousness, the undercurrent is one of bitter desperation and resentment. Uncouth and braggardly, Mark's drunken savagery is relieved only by the interplay of the other characters, for example in his Scottish uncle's remark that 'At the risk of being thought an epicure ... I maun say I'd like my wine handled more tenderly'. Throughout the novel there is a sullenness in Mark O'Donoghue which can scarcely be considered attractive, but in the causes of this ill-humour and in his attempts to overcome it we discover the qualities which ultimately make him a character of considerably more depth and interest than the novelist's previous heroes.

Since the novel is essentially the story of his development, of the growth of his self-knowledge, the reader is bound to ask the question, is Mark simply the shuttlecock of his own passions and of a malign fate or does he possess the nobility of the impassioned and committed revolutionary? That the rebellion itself is given only a very cursory examination does not detract from the importance of the question, and chapter by chapter, piece by piece, Lever gives us the information which once accumulated enables us to formulate an answer. The very fact that the information is provided in this piece-meal fashion constitutes one of the great strengths of the novel. Our impressions are not dictated by the intrusive interpretations of an omniscient author; insights are, of course, provided, but it is in the sequence of Mark's own thoughts, words and actions – particularly in relation to his cousin Kate – that the clues to his character are to be discovered.

From the very outset, Mark is the subject of misapprehensions which fuel his hatred and distrust of the English and go far to reinforce his awareness of his ambiguous position in relation to all about him. The novel opens with the first confrontation of the scion of the ancient owners of the land and its new possessor and, in its mutual misunderstandings, the meeting augers ill for the future. Misinterpreting Mark's apparel, Sir Marmaduke addresses him as one of his tenants:

'I say, my good fellow, what does that smoke mean we see yonder?'
 The youth sprang to his feet with a bound that almost startled his questioner, so sudden and abrupt the motion; his features, inactive and colourless the moment before, seemed almost convulsed now, while they became dark with blood.

'Was it to me you spoke?' said he, in a low, guttural tone, which his passion made actually tremulous.[7]

Although the situation is defused by the tact of Sir Marmaduke's daughter, Sybella, the seeds of dislike and resentment are sown and Mark is quick to point out to the Englishman the difference between hereditary and legal rights, as they apply to the land upon which they stand:

'This belongs to an Englishman – a certain Sir Marmaduke Travers – it is the estate of O'Donoghue.'
'Was, you mean, once,' answered the old man, quickly.[8]

Mark is one of 'the survivors of the old landed class, pushed down the scale to subtenants, but retaining more status than often supposed'[9] – and more pride of 'family'. His resentment is fed by an unassailable belief in the O'Donoghues' absolute right to a living from the land which they have inhabited for generations. The antagonism which finds such early expression is further fuelled by non-political rivalry when Kate O'Donoghue returns from the Low Countries. Awed by his cousin's manifest talent and beauty, Mark is dumb-struck and can only witness in mute jealousy and anger the budding rapport between Kate and Sir Marmaduke's son, Frederick.

In first describing Mark, Lever takes pains to point out that although his hero is dissatisfied with his lot, his discontent is impotent and can find no means of expression other than in sullen obstinacy and a quickness to resentment. His natural strength of character is crippled by an 'utter listlessness and vacuity'. Though blaming the English for the plight of his family, it is sexual jealousy that leads Mark into action of a political or revolutionary nature. Having observed the first meeting on Irish soil between Frederick Travers and Kate O'Donoghue, and having exchanged insults with the former, Mark leaves the castle:

his passion had become almost ungovernable – the entrance of his cousin Kate had but dammed up the current of his anger – and, during the few moments he still remained afterwards, his temper was fiercely tried by witnessing the courtesy of her manner to the stranger, and the apparent intimacy which subsisted between them. 'I ought to have known it,' was the expression he uttered over and over to himself – 'I ought to have known it . . . Curses be on them! they carry persecution through everything – house, home, country, rank, wealth, station – ay, the very affection of our kindred they grudge us! Was slavery ever like this?'[10]

Only through the translation of his sexual energy is Mark at last able to become politically active. On being told by Lanty Lawler of the imminent rising, in his rage he rashly pledges his service in the cause of the United Irishmen:

'I'm with you, whatever comes of it . . . I'm with you; and if the rest have as little to live for, trust me, they'll not be pleasant adversaries.'[11]

Without the catalyst of his jealousy it is doubtful whether Mark's potential for action would have attained even the semblance of direction.

As the novel progresses and Mark's involvement with the rebellion deepens, his patriotism discovers new means to express itself. Although the causes of his original pledge remain distinctly questionable the sincerity of his commitment is soon beyond doubt. The web of his relationships with the other main characters does not attain either the simplicity or certainty of his political credo. The discovery of Frederick Travers's moral rectitude further complicates Mark's feelings concerning the romantic liaison which he believes to exist between the Englishman and Kate, since he can no longer dismiss his rival as a despoiler lacking in both worth and honour:

> Mark dropped his head, and uttered not a word. He could better have looked on Travers wounded and bleeding than have seen him thus elevated above himself by temper and manly candour. The vengeance he had yearned after so long was not only snatched from his grasp, but in the bitterness of disappointment its sting was turned against himself.[12]

Furthermore, he is to learn that not only has he been betrayed and misled by his fellow United Irishmen but that he has been deceived even by his father, whose financial straits have led him into acts of criminal fraud. Pursued by the authorities and embittered towards all around him, Mark retreats into hiding on the coast where he watches for the landing of the French forces in Bantry Bay:

> Mark waited, as men wait for an event that shall call upon their faculties or their courage for some unusual effort. The same reverses that had taught him distrust, had also inculcated the lesson of patience; but it was the patience of the Indian warrior, who will lie crouching in concealment for days long, till the moment of his vengeance has arrived. And thus, while to others he seemed an altered character, less swayed by rash impulses, and less carried away by anger, the curbed up passions became only more concentrated by repression.[13]

This passage is vital to our understanding of Mark's character. That the events of the novel have transformed him in many particulars is not denied – he has become more thoughtful, more capable of reasoned rather than impetuous action, in his conversation and behaviour more sophisticated, in his self-expression more articulate – but these changes are the polish applied through experience. In essence he is the same man burdened by many of the same innate flaws. Perhaps the most significant step in his development is that he has come to recognise his faults, and in this recognition Lever allows him the prospect of redemption:

A Year of Growth

a mighty change had come over him . . . no mere check of disappointment, no baffled ambition could have done this . . . it was the first step towards freedom of a mind enthralled by its own strong passions.[14]

The characterisation bears the stamp of reality; Mark does not undergo a miraculous transformation – the frog is not turned by some feat of authorial legerdemain into the handsome prince, and the misunderstandings and doubts between himself and the heroine remain unresolved. Discounting the trite and contrived conclusion dictated by the publisher M'Glashan's deference to the supposed requirements of his female readership, we last see Mark making his dramatic bid to reach a French man-o'-war as the fleet, in the teeth of a terrific storm, leaves the bay and Ireland to its fate:

> Seated on the deck, silent and thoughtful, Mark seemed indifferent to the terrible storm, whose violence increased every moment, and as the vessel tacked beneath the tall cliffs, when every heart beat anxiously, and every eye was fixed on the stern rocks above them, his glance was calm, and his pulse was tranquil; he felt as though fate had done her worst, and that the future had no heavier blow in store for him.[15]

Having witnessed the wreck of his hopes for liberation – hopes which may have been supported by little more than a desperate tenacity – Mark decides to abandon Ireland and 'never go back'.

One of Lever's greatest traits as a novelist is his ability to engage for his creations the ungrudging sympathy of his readers, and *The O'Donoghue* is no exception to this general rule. The progressive characterisation of his hero and the clearly described duality of his motivation in rebellion make compelling reading, and Mark's departure from his native shores amidst the tumult of a maritime storm provides a fitting ending to a novel which has charted the career of its headstrong and impassioned protagonist.

– III –

In an oft quoted letter addressed to Maria Edgeworth in 1846, Lever stated:

> I have no constructiveness in my head; the most I am capable of is the portraiture of certain characters with more or less of contrast of 'relief' between them. These once formed, I put them *en scene*, to die out in an early chapter when their vitality is weak – if stronger, to survive to the end of the volume.[16]

The justice of this self-criticism can be easily verified by reference to some of his weaker novels, *Sir Brook Fossbrooke*, for instance, in which characters appear and disappear with a head-spinning rapidity; but this fault cannot be found in *The O'Donoghue*. In a writer with so little 'constructiveness', and one who laboured under the disadvantages of serial composition, it is surprising that there is no redundancy. Every character introduced has a role to play – and while the modern reader might feel well able to dispense with the services of such light-weight romantic inventions as Herbert O'Donoghue and Sybella Travers, their being surplus to requirement would not have been so obvious to a Victorian readership accustomed to such conventional heroes and heroines. In themselves they do not compare particularly unfavourably with many a Dickensian creation. The application of such a sparing hand in populating the story, coupled with the novel's remarkable dearth of narrative digressions, further illustrates a new artistic integrity in Lever's approach to his work.

That he felt satisfied with the outcome of his efforts is perhaps best displayed in his decision to borrow quite freely from *The O'Donoghue* when composing his final and – according to many critics – his best novel, *Lord Kilgobbin*. In discussing *Lord Kilgobbin*, A. Norman Jeffares states that 'the politics of the novel are wide-embracing. They are the result of the interactions of the policies of Westminster and Dublin Castle, on the one hand, and those of a complex, changing Ireland on the other'.[17] With certain reservations, the same claim might be made for the earlier novel. In the twenty-seven years between the two works Lever had led a 'full, robustly varied life' and had become a servant of the state, serving as Vice-consul in Spezzia and Consul in Trieste; this wealth of experience had naturally done much to strengthen 'the authority of the novelist as narrator'.[18] His handling of the political side of his matter is far more mature in the later work and his confidence in his abilities is reflected in his willingness to allow the politics to play a far more prominent role in its development, contrasting with their relatively subservient function in *The O'Donoghue*. But a political thread runs through the course of the earlier book, and in both novels there is an attempt to reveal the varied viewpoints of the government and native parties. In *The O'Donoghue* the opposing sides are represented on the one hand by the family of Sir Marmaduke Travers and on the other by Mark O'Donoghue, whilst in *Lord Kilgobbin* the two factions are headed by Cecil Walpole, private secretary to the Lord Lieutenant, and by the Fenian, Daniel Donogan. Government ineptitude is highlighted in both works. In *The O'Donoghue* it is the failure of the authorities to take the threat of invasion seriously and to instead embroil themselves in the petty intricacies of party politics:

A Year of Growth

While they who meditated the invasion of Ireland were thoroughly informed on the state of parties and the condition of public opinion in that kingdom, the English Government were satisfied with vague and insufficient rumours of those intentions, derived from sources of questionable accuracy, or communicated by persons in the pay of their opponents. Certain it is, neither the magnitude of the peril was appreciated, nor its nearness suspected. . . .

a few scattered facts, ill-authenticated and vague, were all that our Government attained to; and even these were unattended to, save when they implicated the conduct of some suspected character nearer home; then, indeed, party violence assumed an appearance of statesmanlike vigilance, and Crown prosecutions and *ex-officio* informations seemed the safeguard of the empire.[19]

In *Lord Kilgobbin*, Lever is able to benefit from a lifetime of experience and a careful observation of the changing condition of Ireland in his satirical condemnation of government policy towards the province:

The Premier was about, as newspapers call it, 'to inaugurate a new policy,' and he wanted a man who knew nothing about Ireland . . . The Minister, however, wanted more than mere ignorance: he wanted that sort of indifference on which a character for impartiality could so easily be constructed. Not alone a man un-acquainted with Ireland, but actually incapable of being influenced by an Irish motive or affected by an Irish view of anything.[20]

While the whole of the later novel is marked by an incisive appreciation of political and diplomatic life which can come only from practical experience, in his early work Lever exhibits the germ of a political understanding which, in its fully developed form, he would later allow to become the foundation of perhaps his greatest work of fiction.

There are other similarities between the two novels, in the all-pervading gloom which shrouds them both, for instance, or in their settings, which reflect the overall narrative tone. As Chris Morash has pointed out, *Lord Kilgobbin* 'moves back and forth between a world of abundance and destitution';[21] so too does *The O'Donoghue*, contrasting the natural abundance of the valley of Glenflesk with its rugged and barren hinterland. In its description the valley seems almost a paradise:

In all the luxuriance of this mild climate, shrubs attained the height of trees; and flowers, rare enough elsewhere to demand the most watchful care, grew here, unattended and unregarded. The very grass had a depth of green, softer and more pleasing to the eye than in other places. It seemed as if nature had, in compensation for the solitude around, shed her fairest gifts over this lonely spot.[22]

But it is a paradise inhabited by the English Travers family, while the O'Donoghues – the land's ancient masters – dwell, like post-lapsarian outcasts, at its gates. While Sir Marmaduke enjoys every luxury, his Irish counterparts can muster only a semblance of gentility. The ancient castles of both the O'Donoghue and Lord Kilgobbin reflect the fallen condition of their fortunes; that of the former is described as a 'strange, incongruous pile, in which fortress and farm-house seemed welded together', while Kilgobbin Castle bears the same stamp of decay:

> On this border-land between fertility and destitution, and on a tract which had probably once been part of the bog itself, there stood – there stands still – a short, square tower, battlemented at top, and surmounted with a pointed roof, which seems to grow out of a cluster of farm-buildings, so surrounded is its base by roofs of thatch and slates. Incongruous, vulgar, and ugly in every way, the old keep appears to look down on them – time-worn and battered as it is – as might a reduced gentleman regard the unworthy associates with which an altered fortune had linked him.[23]

The structural uncertainty of their respective domiciles is a reflection of the social ambiguity in which both men find themselves. The O'Donoghue continues to be revered by his tenantry while being an object of amusement to those whom he would consider his peers; the dubiousness of his claim to nobility makes Lord Kilgobbin's doubtful social standing even more pronounced, and in his subtle development of this device of separation we can see the growth of Lever's skill as a novelist.

Further similarities can be found in the chief heroines of the two novels, Kate O'Donoghue and Nina Kostalergi, and in their fates. A comparison of the two girls reveals so many shared characteristics that it is impossible not to conclude that Lever was thinking of the one whilst creating the other. Both girls are of mixed blood and are introduced as outsiders to the family circle and both produce a galvanic effect on their previously apathetic hosts. No less electrifying are their political opinions. Of Kate O'Donoghue, Lever states:

> How often she wished she had been a boy – how many a day-dream floated before her of such a career as she might have struck out! Ireland a nation – her 'own sons her rulers' – had been the theme of many an oft-heard tale; and there was a poetry in the sentiment of a people recalled to a long-lost, long-sought-for nationality, that excited and exalted her imagination.[24]

Opinions of a like nature are held by Nina Kostalergi, though her expression of them follows much more closely the idioms of everyday thought and conversation:

> 'the mere permission to live under a bad government is too high a price to pay for life at all. I'd rather go "Down into the streets," as they call it, and have it out, than I'd drudge on, dogged by policemen, and sent to gaol on suspicion.'
> 'He is right,' cried Nina. 'If I were a man, I'd think as he does.'[25]

In practically every detail, even down to their foreign pronunciation of English, Kate is the forerunner of Nina. Most obviously of all, both girls

A Year of Growth

at last link their fortunes with the insurgent heroes. Kate and Mark are not bound together until the rather redundant and anti-climactic final pages of *The O'Donoghue* whereas Nina's elopement with Donogan provides the perfect *denouement* in *Lord Kilgobbin*, but surely the fate of the earlier heroine suggested that of the later.

In comparing their many points of similarity – in tone, setting, characterisation and theme – we can identify *The O'Donoghue* as the blueprint of Lever's most mature work. But, to many readers, the comparison will not necessarily be all in favour of *Lord Kilgobbin*. In writing the later novel, Lever was able to benefit from twenty-seven years' worth of maturity and experience but these assets were purchased at the expense of a dramatic exuberance which, though considerably mellowed since the composition of *Harry Lorrequer* and *Charles O'Malley*, is still very much present in *The O'Donoghue*. *Lord Kilgobbin* is perhaps Lever's most consistently dour work of fiction with the author making practically no effort to counterbalance the all-pervading gloom. The atmosphere of *The O'Donoghue* is also dark but there is a dramatic impetus which to some degree alleviates the narrative despondency. Throughout the novel there is a series of incidents which, though occasionally leaning towards melodrama, acts as a very successful spur for the reader's interest. Most dramatic of all is the concluding series of chapters in which event follows rapidly upon event, with Mark's dramatic departure from Ireland providing the climax. Admittedly some of Lever's devices have not withstood the test of time: the Macchiavellian convolutions of the agent, Hemsworth, for instance, but even these are to some degree redeemed by the overall credibility of the villain's characterisation.

– IV –

That Lever himself knew *The O'Donoghue* to be a considerable advance upon his earlier work and that he had taken greater pains with its composition we know from his spirited defence of the book when some critics accused him of advocating Repeal and a desertion of the traditionally Tory stance of the *Dublin University Magazine*:

> With the little ability I can command, I have tried to bring Irish gentlemen into better repute, not by exaggerated pictures of good qualities so much as by correct delineation of the state of the society in which they live, where there are abundant apologies for many failings; and also by pictures of a country where, whatever its faults, most of the best features have their origin in the native high-mindedness, cordial warmth, and general good-feeling of the Irish gentleman.[26]

There is ample evidence that he felt the criticisms of this work to be particularly unjust and depressing. It was a matter of considerable consequence to him that one of his great literary icons, Maria Edgeworth, should write to him to express her own appreciation of the novel, and in speaking of her letter Lever stated to his friend Alexander Spencer that 'I never made such an effort as in this book'.[27]

If we accept that in *The O'Donoghue* there is to be discovered a new Charles Lever, a writer whose attitudes and style have undergone momentous changes, what were the causes of this development? Can any particular catalyst be identified which produced these changes, or were they simply the result of a natural self-generating progression? The answer probably lies somewhere between the two possibilities. In writing his 1872 preface to *Charles O'Malley*, he stated that:

> The ease with which I strung my stories together ... led me to believe that I could draw on this vein of composition without any limit whatever. I felt, or thought I felt, an inexhaustible store of fun and buoyancy within me.[28]

By the end of his career Lever was able to acknowledge that this confidence was mistaken and that his fund of drollery was far from unlimited. His sense of humour never deserted him and in his maturity he could still write a comedy of very great merit, *The Dodd Family Abroad*, but the humour of this book, and its means of expression, are very different from that of his first forays into fiction. It is clear that his prodigality in the creation of *Harry Lorrequer*, *Charles O'Malley* and *Arthur O'Leary* (1844) had gone far to exhaust his funds not only of drollery but of 'buoyancy' also and that unless he was to satisfy himself with ghostly and feeble imitations of his earliest work something new must be attempted.

But there were other influences at work. In October 1843 William Carleton published an article in *The Nation* in which he indicted Lever on charges of writing for an English audience at the expense of the Irish peasantry – the first criticism in which Lever's name is linked with the stigma of the 'stage-Irishman'. On an earlier occasion, in 1836, Carleton had revealed an hostility to Lever, when he accused him of plagiarism in a story entitled 'The Black Mask' – the incident eventually being explained by the duplicity of a literary agent employed by Lever.[29] Despite this early clash Lever evinced respect and admiration for Carleton, asking M'Glashan, in a communication concerning *Harry Lorrequer*:

> No comparison with my friend Carleton, I beseech you – so far, so very far, indeed, beyond the standard by which I could wish anything of mine measured.[30]

Although we have no record of his actual response to Carleton's article, in the light of his obvious appreciation of the latter's work, it is not too much to suppose that he would have taken the review in *The Nation* very seriously. With hindsight, with the knowledge that as he wrote his rollicking novels of fun and mayhem, Ireland teetered on the brink of a disaster of unprecedented proportions, we might well acknowledge the justice of Carleton's attack. But we should remember that in his early days Lever was making no claims to be anything other than an entertainer:

> I began to have a misty, half confused impression that Englishmen generally laboured under a sad-coloured temperament, took depressing views of life, and were proportionately grateful to any one who would rally them even passingly, out of their despondency.[31]

He had taken up his pen because he needed money, and it seemed that the most money was to be earned by the writer who could make his audience laugh. Dickens had learned this same lesson, and the audience for which Lever wrote was identical with the one which had taken to its heart the creator of *The Pickwick Papers* (1839). That Lever had embarked upon his writing career for purely mercenary conditions was not unusual – Thackeray's motivation was far from dissimilar – but where he differed from many of his contemporaries was in his growing beyond these limitations and, at the risk of alienating his hitherto loyal audience, launching out into a very different kind of fiction. True, financial gain remained a vital consideration, and he can be criticised for continuing to make a number of artistic compromises at the instigation of his publishers, but in writing *The O'Donoghue*, he should be given credit for responding positively to both his own internal promptings and to the criticism of his peers.

– V –

Critical opinion concerning *St Patrick's Eve* is unanimously in favour of this short work. Certainly, it has a vital role to play in any attempt to defend Lever against the criticisms of his Nationalist detractors, and there is no ambiguity over his intentions when writing it:

> I desired to inculcate the truth, that prosperity has as many duties as adversity has sorrows; that those to whom Providence has accorded many blessings are but the stewards of His bounty to the poor; and that the neglect of an obligation so sacred as this charity is a grievous wrong.[32]

The novel is a straightforward description of the horrors of poverty and the concomitant evils of hunger and disease. In its composition Lever made use of his first-hand knowledge of the cholera epidemic of 1832, during which it was not unknown for the doctors themselves to heave into the coffins their unfortunate patients. The scenes which he witnessed made a lasting impression on the young physician and his descriptions in *St Patrick's Eve* bear the powerful stamp of actual experience:

> The cart moved on, and at length stopped at a small hovel built against the side of a clay ditch. It was a mere assemblage of wet sods with the grass still growing . . . Owen halted the ass at the opening of the miserable den, through which the smoke now issued, and at the same moment a man, stooping double to permit him to pass out into the open air, came forward: he was apparently about fifty years of age – his real age was not thirty; originally a well-formed and stout-built fellow, starvation and want had made him a mere skeleton . . . he had neither hat, shoes, nor stockings; but still, all these signs of destitution were nothing in comparison with the misery displayed in his countenance. Except that his lip trembled with a convulsive shiver, not a feature moved – the cheeks were livid and flattened – the dull grey eyes had lost all the light of intelligence, and stared vacantly before him.[33]

Despite the brutal realism of his depiction of the dehumanising effects of destitution and infection, Lever makes his admiration of the peasantry abundantly clear. For his hero he does not choose a representative of the landlord class, but Owen Connor, 'the very ideal of an Irish peasant of the west'. It is with the effects of landlord absenteeism on the essentially noble peasants of Owen's class that Lever is primarily concerned. As Richard Haslam explains, by leaving the ground on which their responsibility centres the landlords are guilty not only of a moral laxity but of a political short-sightedness which will eventually cost them their estates:

> The moral failure of the landowners accompanies a lack of pragmatic, *realpolitik* insight. The collapse of the social compact, set into motion by their neglect or absence during the epidemic, will eventually destroy them.[34]

Despite the realism of its description, and the impassioned and sincere tone of its argument, however, *St Patrick's Eve* evinces a naiveté and a tendency to over-simplification in its insistence that the evils experienced by the Irish peasant would be almost universally remedied by the return to their estates of the landlords. In defending his book Lever stated:

> I wrote what I believe to be the truth in *St Patrick* . . . if I should live and am able to work out my intention, I will recur to the topic, and certainly not spare the owners of property who prefer factious political influence to a position of credit and honour, and self-indulgence to the high duties of their station.[35]

He identifies the 1800 Act of Union and the subsequent provincialisation of Dublin as the main causes for landlord absenteeism but, despite its moral authority, his appeal to the landlords' sense of duty was almost certain to prove futile without a simultaneous call for political reform. Furthermore, his examination of the causes of absenteeism is essentially a cursory one. In *Modern Ireland*, R.F. Foster offers a more detailed analysis of the reasons for the landowners' absence and, while he refers specifically to absenteeism in the eighteenth century, his reappraisal serves to shed light on the circumstances prevalent in the nineteenth:

The general picture of absentee landlords living an easy life off exorbitant rent-rolls needs qualification... There could also be special reasons for absenteeism: some Catholic landlords found it necessary rather than convenient. Careers in the army, the diplomatic corps and English politics provided further causes. And some lived away from their estates not in order to spend money but to save it.[36]

Despite Lever's belief that *St Patrick's Eve* constituted his *mot sur l'Irelande*,[37] his failure to fully understand the underlying causes of social disintegration considerably weakens the novel. The impact of the Act of Union is given a more full and rounded treatment in *The Knight of Gwynne*, but the novelist's growing awareness of the unacceptability of facile and over-simplified generalisations and the inapplicability to 'Irish' novels of the conventional 'happy ending' finds its fullest expression in his later cholera novel: *The Martins of Cro' Martin*.

Phiz's original half title to *The Knight of Gwynne* (1847). While Phiz illustrated the majority of Lever's novels, the relationship between artist and writer was not always an easy one. Phiz's obvious delight in capturing moments of intense comic vibrancy was well suited to such novels as *Charles O'Malley* (1841) and *The Dodd Family Abroad* (1854), but accorded less well with novels of increasing seriousness and reduced vitality.

3

AN INIQUITOUS ACT

– I –

Late in 1845, Lever started work on his first full-length novel for his new publishers, Chapman and Hall. His hitherto successful and lucrative relationship with Curry and Co and their representative, James M'Glashan, had drawn to an acrimonious conclusion amidst arguments over money, the publisher's over-sensitive reaction to Tory criticism of *The O'Donoghue*, and over 'hints of a deep intrigue on the M'Glashan side to injure' the author's dealings with the London publishers.[1] His relationship with the *Dublin University Magazine* continued for some years, but Curry and Co were to publish no more of his books after 1845. Although frustrated and angered by the episode, Lever was buoyed up by the new partnership and by the magnificent financial rewards which it promised. The relationship which began with such high hopes would last for some twenty years, with Chapman and Hall remaining his publisher almost exclusively until 1865.[2]

J.A. Sutherland has identified the commencement of the new work, *The Knight of Gwynne*, as a defining moment:

at the critically testing point of his career, [Lever] did make the break for artistic freedom. . . . This was clearly his great chance. *The Knight of Gwynne* is a complete departure from the rollicking military tales he had hitherto specialised in. A political story centred on the Union between England and Ireland it was designed to reflect current concerns and to contribute something serious to the debate on repeal. (It also indicates an intended challenge to Dickens as the leading novelist of social conscience.)[3]

In his last full length novel, *The O'Donoghue*, Lever had examined, albeit rather obliquely, the events leading up to the 1798 rebellion. His decision to treat the 1800 Act of Union in his next work seems a perfectly natural progression for any novelist conducting an exploration of modern Irish historical themes, particularly in light of the common perception that the Act was a direct response to the incendiary activities of the Young Irishmen:

> constitutional union between Ireland and England seems a logical consequence of the 1798 rebellion: a structural answer to the Irish problem, with overtones of 'moral assimilation' and expectations that an infusion of English manners would moderate sectarianism.[4]

When we consider that his next novel in this 'series', *The Martins of Cro' Martin*, concerns itself with the 1829 Catholic Emancipation Act, the progression appears planned and coherent.

In passing the government sponsored Act of Union, the members of the Irish parliament seated at College Green effectively voted themselves out of a job, and their countrymen out of their independently elected parliamentary representation:

> The new system abolished the Irish parliament, while retaining the Castle government. The representation of Irish constituencies was to be transferred to Westminster, with the representatives carefully restricted to one hundred. The number of boroughs was cut down, with compensation to patrons; the counties remained as two-member constituencies; the Irish peers elected twenty-eight of their body to sit in the Lords, along with four Irish bishops.[5]

To many Irishmen, both at the time and afterwards, the Union was seen as the final act of British encroachment on Irish liberty and as a symbol of the willingness of many Ascendancy politicians to prostitute themselves for the wealth and position which only the government could confer. Born six years after the passing of the Act, Lever saw it in precisely these terms. In fact, as R.F. Foster indicates, there was a wide variance between the actual and perceived results of the Union:

> The fact of the Union was to set rhetorical terms of nationalist politics over the next century: and this has led to some reluctance to confront the question of how much difference it actually made. Apart from the absence of the College Green assembly, changes were ostensibly minimal – which may be a reflection of the limited nature of that assembly itself. The government of Ireland, far from being integrated with that of Britain, remained a special case.[6]

Nationalist commentators have viewed the Act as an infringement of Irish political liberties and independence; it was viewed in exactly the same way by the Ascendancy politicians who opposed it, and indeed by Lever himself. During the 1840s, the time at which he wrote *The Knight of Gwynne*, the debate over the repeal of the Union was at its height and the novel forms his contribution to it. However, like so many Ascendancy sympathisers who considered the Union a mistake, Lever was opposed to repeal. He intended that his condemnatory description and analysis of the movement towards, and immediate aftermath of Union should, at the same time, demonstrate the impossibility of repeal. An understanding of the strength of Ascendancy opposition to repeal – an opposition which might, ostensibly, appear to be in direct contradiction of its original objection to the Act – is central to an understanding of Lever's work and attitudes and, more broadly, to an understanding of the predicament of the Ascendancy in the nineteenth century.

– II –

Like many Irishmen, Lever saw the Act of Union as a betrayal of Ireland's constitutional liberty; though, of course, political independence had rested solely with the Protestant Ascendancy. With the passing of the 1829 Catholic Emancipation Act, however, any Irish parliament resulting from repeal would be very different from the pre-Union institution. Catholics could now be elected to parliament and could hold most high offices; the days of Protestant domination of any Irish parliament were effectively over. For this reason alone, most of the Irish Protestants who bemoaned the Union, including Lever, opposed repeal. In contrast, many Catholics had supported Union in the belief that it would be an important step towards enfranchisement; emancipation having been achieved they were anxious to exercise their new power in an Irish assembly and therefore advocated repeal under the leadership of Daniel O'Connell.

Upon commencing *The Knight of Gwynne*, Lever confirmed the seriousness of his intent, at the same time identifying his chosen targets:

I have a great object in view – no less than to show that the bribed men of the Irish Parliament are the very men who now are joining the Liberal ranks, and want to assist O'Connell in bringing back the Parliament they once sold, and would sell again if occasion offered.[7]

To him, as to many others, the most pernicious result of the Union was the subsequent marginalisation of an Ireland robbed of its political independence and deserted by a gentry which now saw the English parliament as the sphere in which it might exert its political influence. The fear that Ireland would be left to the mercy of an ambitious under-class is articulated by the eponymous hero of the novel, the enormously wealthy and aristocratic member of the Irish parliament, Maurice Darcy:

'Do not tell me, my lord, that we shall hold our station in the Imperial Parliament. There are many reasons against such a belief. We shall be in the minority, a great minority; a minority branded with provincialism as our badge, and accused of prejudice and narrow-sightedness, from the very fact of our nationality. No, no; we shall occupy a very different position in your country; and who will take our places here? ... The demagogue, the public disturber, the licensed hawker of small grievances, every briefless lawyer of bad fortune and worse language, every mendicant patriot that can minister to the passions of a people deserted by their natural protectors – the day will come, my lord, when these men will grow ambitious, their aspirings may become troublesome; if you coerce them, they are martyrs – conciliate them, and they are privileged. What will happen then? You will be asked to repeal the Union, you will be charged with all the venality by which you carried your bill, every injustice with which it is chargeable, and with a hundred other faults and crimes with which it is unconnected. You will be asked, I say, to repeal the Union, and make of this miserable rabble, these dregs and sweepings of Party, a Parliament... You will be asked to repeal the Union, to give a Parliament to a country which you have drained of its wealth, from which you have seduced the aristocracy; to restore a deliberative body to a land whose resources for self-legislation you have studiously and industriously ruined.'[8]

It is here that the events of the Union are used by Lever to comment upon events taking place at the time of his writing. He devotes some space to a description of how this under-class developed itself into a 'party' or, perhaps more accurately, parties. He intended that his description should act as a warning to his contemporary audience and to those contemplating repeal. Believing that Union had weakened Ireland, he also felt that repeal nearly forty years on would place the country and its people in the hands of those who, instead of rebuilding its strength, would manipulate it for their own selfish ends.

Despite his opposition to the Union, it is not the bill's supporters who are the primary targets for Lever's criticism. Rather, it is the equivocators and manipulators who are attacked. Chief among the equivocators is Hickman O'Reilly, son of Dr Hickman, an apothecary and usurer made almost monstrous by the combination of avariciousness and extreme old age. While Dr Hickman seeks only to add to his already enormous wealth, accumulated through money-lending and the astute acquirement of over-ripe mortgages on encumbered properties, O'Reilly's ambition is to be accepted as a member of the gentry and to ensure social ascendancy. They engineer the Knight's ruination through the manipulation of his corrupted agent, Tom Gleeson, and, albeit temporarily, overturn the established order in precisely the manner predicted by the Knight for the whole of Ireland. The Ascendancy landlord is reduced to near-penury while the bourgeois of low-birth is raised to influence and wealth.

O'Reilly is seen to lack any political scruple or conviction: his one aim is to secure his position in the country. As with Marion Bramleigh in the later *The Bramleighs of Bishop's Folly*, he believes that the advancement of a family from obscurity to social ascendancy is to be achieved through gradual progression: from wealth, to power attained through the use of this wealth, to security in station through intermarriage. Wealth and station have already been achieved – O'Reilly has a seat in parliament – but the government's willingness to purchase support for the Union Bill with extensive bribery, including the granting of office and titles, offers him a further opportunity. With many others, Lever believed that the bribery practised by the government was exceptional. This was not, in fact, the case, though its scale was unprecedented:

> Jobs, places and peerages were created with an energy that brought the mechanisms for executive control of the legislature to their *reductio ad absurdum*. Contemporary conventions were observed more punctiliously than is sometimes allowed: there was much agonizing over what was, and was not, correct practice in purchasing support. But in the end, the operation tended to degenerate into a trade in 'borough stock'.[9]

While the chief-mover in the government's strategy, Lord Castlereagh, is treated with remarkable sympathy by Lever, the strategy itself is held up to opprobrium, as are its prey, in the form of such individuals as O'Reilly:

> There seemed a kind of panic abroad. Men feared to walk without the protective mantle of the Crown being extended over them; the barriers of shame were broken down by the extent to which corruption had spread. The examples of infamy were many, and several were reconciled to the ignominy of their degradation by their associates in disgrace. That in such general corruption the judgements of the public should have been equally wholesale, is little to be wondered at; the regret is rather that they were so rarely unjust and ill-bestowed.
> Public confidence was utterly uprooted; there was a national bankruptcy of honour and none were trusted.[10]

It is in this climate that O'Reilly, when he fails to obtain the baronetcy which he craves, seats himself on the opposition, 'Patriot' benches and thereby earns the adulation of the masses. His cynical adoption of Nationalist symbolism – he decks-out his footmen in 'emerald green,' while 'an Irish motto ornamented the garter of the family crest[11] – underlines his, and by implication his class', unscrupulous willingness to manipulate circumstances for their own benefit. At precisely the time when O'Reilly is being acclaimed as a man of the people, the Knight's actions have condemned him to scorn and ridicule. By first dining with Castlereagh and by then failing to vote on the Union Bill, as a result of debilitating shock at the sudden announcement of his ruin, the Knight has left himself open to accusations of having been 'bought' by the government party.

Chief among the government's agents and 'manipulators' is Con Heffernan. Heffernan uses bribery and corruption, deceit and half-promises as the tools of his trade. Eschewing actual political office, he instead prefers to make himself essential to those who, however transiently, hold it:

> 'Reflect, for a moment, what kind of thing the government of Ireland is; see the difficulty, nay, the impossibility of any set of men arriving here fresh from England being able to find out their way, or make any guess at the leading characters about them: every retiring official likes to embarrass his successor – that's all natural and fair; then, what a mass of blunders and mistakes await the newly-come Viceroy or Secretary! In the midst of the bleak expanse of pathless waste I was the sign-post. The new players, who took up the cards when the game was half over, could know nothing of what trumps were in, or what tricks were taken. I was there to tell them all; they soon saw that I could do this; and they also saw that I wanted nothing from any party.'[12]

Revelling in his skill, rather than in the material rewards that the skill can win, Heffernan is the arch-Macchiavel. Supreme confidence in his abilities, joined with a knowledge of the foibles of his 'victims', render him a dangerous opponent. Although he is unable to utilise his particular talents to suborn the Knight, and although he finds himself at one point duped into unconsciously abetting the schemes of Hickman O'Reilly, Heffernan falls victim to his own success rather than to the wiles of another. Behind the scenes, he has worked indefatigably for the Union; when the bill is passed, however, he becomes redundant. His unique talents and influence are suddenly surplus to requirements and his chief-sponsor, Castlereagh, upon promotion to the Cabinet loses all interest in his doings:

> Like most men who cultivate mere cunning, he underrated all who do not place the greatest reliance upon it, and in this way conceived a very depreciating estimate of Lord Castlereagh's ability. Knowing how deeply he had himself been trusted, and how much employed in state transactions, he speculated on a long career of political influence, and that, while his lordship remained as Secretary, his own skill and dexterity would never be dispensed with. This pleasant illusion was now dispelled, and he saw his speculations scattered to the winds at once; in fact, to borrow his own sagacious illustration, 'he had to submit to a new deal with his hand full of trumps.'[13]

Castlereagh's indifference covers more than Heffernan's activities, it applies equally to all things Irish. Ireland has served its purpose, success there has paved his way to greater achievements to be fulfilled on English soil; with the facile cynicism of the accomplished politician he turns his back upon Ireland and its inhabitants as easily as he cuts his agent adrift. Although Lever's portrait of Castlereagh is largely sympathetic, this act of desertion – far more than the Union itself, perhaps – reinforces and justifies Irish distrust of the English administration. Despite the arguments which he uses to persuade the Knight of the benefits to be experienced by Ireland as a result of the Union, the country and its people serve simply as a stepping-stone in the path of his ambition.

The Act passed and Castlereagh departed, Heffernan attempts to create just the kind of 'underdog' party whose existence was predicted by the Knight as the inevitable spawn of Union. By actively creating an atmosphere in which cupidity not only thrives, but is actively encouraged, and by making the capital unappealing to the country's 'natural protectors', the government has left it a prey to another band of self-seekers:

'To make Ireland ungovernable without us must be our aim and object – to embarrass and confound every administration – to oppose the Ministers – pervert their good objects and exaggerate their bad. Pledged to no distinct line of acting, we can be patriotic when it suits us, and declaim on popular rights when nothing better offers. Acting in concert, and diffusing an influence in every county and town and corporation, what Ministry can long resist us, or what Government anxious for office would refuse to make terms with us?'[14]

Some of this band are from the aspiring middle classes, but a greater portion is made up of those men who see themselves as 'neglected', unduly by-passed during the debate on the Union and the concomitant distribution of bribes: their ambitions for peerages or office unfulfilled. By inference, Lever deliberately identifies these men with the Repealers of his own day and condemns the selfish motivation of both. In their pledge to 'confound every administration', we might see a reflection of the policy of each outgoing administration to leave matters in a state of deliberate confusion. Essentially, Ireland is seen to fall 'from the frying-pan into the fire': with the venality of each party vying in its excesses with that of its rival.

Heffernan is an altogether more interesting and challenging character than O'Reilly; the latter's motivations, while realistic, are essentially commonplace. Heffernan's, meanwhile, are the product of intellectual vanity and the perversion of innate ability. He plays the game for its own sake and self-seekers fall an easy prey to him. When canvassing O'Reilly's vote for the Union, he dangled before him the promise of a baronetcy and Castle-favour. Having discovered that the Union has inevitably denuded his own influence, he again tempts O'Reilly with promises of a political and social ascendancy but, bereft of Castlereagh's patronage, he can no longer deliver with such facility.

– III –

Far more threatening to Lever than the party of malcontents represented by O'Reilly and Heffernan, was that which he believed formed the germ of O'Connell's Repeal Movement. Relations between Lever and O'Connell were permanently antagonistic, with the Liberator actually going so far as to denounce 'Lever as an enemy of his country'.[15] In painting the portrait of Counsellor O'Halloran, 'without family, friends, or fortune, but with lungs of leather, and a ready tongue',[16] the novelist returned the favour, creating a biting and satirical portrait of a brutal but shrewd and ambitious politician. From his first appearance, O'Halloran is made deliberately unsympathetic, defending the cause of the unscrupulous Hickman family who have succeeded in obtaining the Knight's estate through the criminal actions of the latter's land-agent, 'Honest Tom Gleeson'. In his attacks upon the absent Knight – and, by implication, upon the Ascendancy as a whole – O'Halloran berates him as a hardened rack-renter, living a life of luxury upon the misery of his tenants:

> He sketched with a masterly but diabolical ingenuity the whole career of the Knight, representing him at every stage of life as the pampered voluptuary seeking means for fresh enjoyment without a thought of the consequences; he exhibited him dispensing, not the graceful duties of hospitality, but the reckless waste of a tasteless household. . . .
>
> He drew a frightful picture of a suffering and poverty-enslaved tenantry, sinking fast into barbarism from hopelessness – unhappily, no Irishman need depend upon his imagination for the sketch.[17]

While the description of the Knight's extravagance is exaggerated, and made to appear the product of a deliberate and uncaring abuse of his position, its strength is born from its basis in fact. We have witnessed the Knight's astonishing wastefulness and total indifference to the details of estate management. That the picture is also genuinely representative of the widespread condition of the peasantry is confirmed by Lever's statement that the everyday experience of all Irishmen renders imagination unnecessary in picturing the horrors of poverty and neglect.

Lever clearly abhors the tactics employed by O'Halloran, but he does not deny the Counsellor's intelligence or political acumen. The political lobbyist, Con Heffernan, for all his perspicacity, is found to be short-sighted and unable to foresee that the success which he engineers in the Union debate will restrict his own sphere of influence; O'Halloran, on the other hand, in his analysis of the political situation and, most particularly, in his recognition of the power of a 'single principle party' is seen to be an altogether more potent threat:

An Iniquitous Act

'Had you adopted one steadfast line of action, set out with one brief intelligible proposition – I care not what – Slave Emancipation, or Catholic Emancipation, Repeal of Tests Acts, or Parliamentary Reform, any of them – taken your stand on that, and that alone, you must have succeeded. Of course, to do this is a work of time and labour; some men will grow weary and sink by the way, but others take up the burden, and the goal is reached at last. There must be years long of writing and speaking, meeting, declaring, and plotting; you must consent to be thought vulgar and low-minded – ay, and to become so, for active partisans are only to be found in low places. You will be laughed at and jeered, abused, mocked, and derided at first; later on, you will be assailed more powerfully, and more coarsely; but, all this while, your strength is developing, your agencies are spreading. Persuasion will induce some; notoriety others; hopes of advantage many more, to join you. You will then have a press as well as a party, and the very men that sneered at your beginnings will have to respect the persistence and duration of your efforts. I don't care how trumpery the arguments used; I don't value one straw the fallacy of the statements put forward. Let one great question, one great demand for anything be made for some five-and-twenty or thirty years – let the Press discuss, and the Parliament debate it – you are sure of its being accorded in the end.'[18]

For all his accusations of chicanery, Lever could not deny the success of O'Connell's tactics; and, in the ascendancy of O'Halloran over his peers, pays a reluctant tribute to this success.

– IV –

The bleakness of this picture is not much alleviated by the story of the Knight himself. The politically motivated 'middle' class of Ireland is much more sympathetically depicted in the later *The Martins of Cro' Martin*, and the condition of the aristocracy examined much more critically, but even in *The Knight of Gwynne* Lever's Tory attitudes are compromised by an inability to champion the Ascendancy whole-heartedly. While he is lauded as the symbol of 'Old Ireland' with its traditions of hospitality and 'manliness', the Knight is also seen to have brought ruin upon himself and upon his family through reckless over-expenditure and the belief that estate management is below the dignity of a gentleman. Instead of mastering the details of his domestic economy, he leaves all to the skill of his agent, 'Honest Tom Gleeson':

For several years past he had managed all the Knight's estates; and such was the complication and entanglement of the property, loaded with mortgages and rent-charges, embarrassed with dowries and annuities, that nothing short of his admirable skill could have supported the means of that expensive and wasteful mode of life which the Knight insisted on pursuing, and all restriction on which he deemed unfitting his station. If Gleeson represented the urgent necessity of retrenchment, the very word was enough to cut short the negotiation; until, at last, the agent was fain to rest content with the fruits of good management, and merely venture from time to time on a cautious suggestion regarding the immense expense of the Knight's household.[19]

Although Gleeson is introduced as an honest man, and one in whom the trust of his clients is well-placed, the supposed safety of his agency does little to mitigate the charge of fecklessness which might be levelled at the Knight. As with the devious and ill-educated Peter Gill in *Lord Kilgobbin*, Gleeson is the one influence which gives any cohesion to the affairs of his employer; once removed, those affairs fall into disarray. No character who allows another to assume such power over his concerns can be viewed entirely sympathetically, his attitude being, at best, naive and, at worst, recklessly irresponsible. The Knight's impending disaster, largely self-generated as it is, gives his words in defence of the gentry an irony perhaps unintended by Lever; if the irony is intentional, the words resound with a pomposity and self-delusion which ill-accords with what was intended, primarily, as a sympathetic portrait:

'Their rank and education would be the best guarantee for the safety and wisdom of their counsels, their property the best surety for the permanence of the institutions of the State. Suddenly acquired wealth can scarcely be intrusted with political power; it lacks the elements of prudent caution, by which property is maintained as well as accumulated.'[20]

Perhaps realising that the details of his characterisation had denied his hero some of his audience's sympathy, Lever attempts to back-track and to ascribe the Knight's extravagance to an awareness that his style of life gives employment to a vast number of retainers:

Partly from long habit and association, partly from indolence of character, but more than either from a compassionate consideration of those whose livelihood might be impaired by any change in his establishment, the Knight had resisted all suggestion of alteration. He viewed the very peculations around him as vested rights, and the most he could pledge himself to was, that when the present race died out he would not appoint any successors.[21]

Despite Lever's best efforts, however, the attempt fails. When the full extent of Gleeson's perfidy is revealed and the Knight stripped of his enormous wealth, the modern reader, at least, cannot help but feel that he has reaped what he had sown through his own foolishness. Gleeson has forged the signatures of both the Knight and his son, has renewed leases at nominal rents and has ended the entail on portions of the estate, all of which activities have involved the Knight unwittingly in a spiral of ever-increasing debt. Criminal though Gleeson's actions have been, they could not have been perpetrated if the Knight had made any attempt to manage or to even understand the details of his estate. Psychologically more interesting than Lever's attempt to defend his hero, and providing a challenging parallel to the idea that the tenantry sank into 'barbarism from hopelessness', is the suggestion that prodigality in the wider sphere was the result of political pessimism:

> The fatal facility of Irish nature, and the still more ruinous influence of example, hurried men along on this road to ruin, and as political prospects grew darker, a reckless indifference to the future succeeded, in which little care was taken for the morrow, until, at last, thoughtless extravagance became a habit, and moneyed difficulties the lot of almost every family of Ireland.[22]

This suggestion that the prodigality of Irish hospitality was a malaise produced, at least in part, by the cloud of British imperial usurpation, adds an altogether new facet to Lever's early portraits of the squirearchy. Indeed, the interest of this suggestion might impinge upon similar portraits by other, better known, artists.

In common with so many of Lever's heroes, the Knight is an outsider: in a novel ostensibly concerned with the causality and repercussions of the Union, its eponymous hero does not even vote upon the bill in question. Admittedly, it is the revelation of his imminent ruin which prevents him from voting, but when still basking in his wealth and rank he indicated a reluctance to do so; this despite the fact that the country around him remained consumed with this one topic of debate. For all his gentility, nobility of nature and honesty, the Knight is seen as essentially ineffectual; all of the characters who surround him, whether or not politically motivated, have more energy and more direction. In comparison, the Knight is almost effete in his inactivity. At no point does Lever suggest that this separation from events is the product of the Knight's hitherto unassailed security in his affluence, but the inference can be drawn and suggests an interesting contrast with the later perception that the Ascendancy was rendered redundant and overcome with ennui only after the Union ended its political independence.

Despite the significant flaws in his character, however, the Knight remains the hero of the novel. Virtuous, honourable and intelligent, he serves as a mouthpiece for Lever's concerns over the impact of the Union. A number of these concerns find expression in other novels. The effects of landlord absenteeism, for instance, are examined in detail in *St Patrick's Eve*, but they are tied most closely to the Union in *The Knight of Gwynne*:

> 'The legitimate influence of the landed gentry is the safeguard of the State; but if, by the attractions of power, the flatteries of a Court, or the seductions of Party, you withdraw them from the rightful sphere of its exercise, you reduce them to

the level of the Borough members, without, perhaps, their technical knowledge or professional acquirements. I am for giving them a higher position – the heritage of the bold barons, from whom they are descended; but to maintain this, they must live on their own estates, dispense the influences of their wealth and their morals in their own native districts, be the friend of the poor man, the counsellor of the misguided, the encourager of the weak; know and be known to all around, not as the corrupt dispensers of Government patronage, but the guardians of those whose rights are in their keeping for defence and protection.'[23]

Like many others of his generation, Lever believed that the Union resulted in the desertion of Ireland by its gentry and in the consequential economic decline. Furthermore, since the gentry provided a moral centre to society, its absence produced a spiritual vacuum which, he clearly believed, remained permanently unfilled. This moral degeneration was exacerbated by the influence of Castle life, with its advocacy of cupidity, and by the gradual influx of English customs and attitudes:

'Oh! sir, believe me, there is a weighty load of responsibility on those who rule us; these things are less the faults of individuals than of a system. You began here by confiscation, you would finish by corruption. Stimulating to excesses of every kind a people ten times more excitable than your own – now flattering, now goading – teaching them to vie with you in display while you mocked the recklessness of their living, you chafed them into excesses of alternate loyalty or rebellion.'[24]

As J.A. Sutherland points out, Phiz's covers for *The Knight of Gwynne* proclaim the good fortune of an Ireland, '"GREAT, GLORIOUS AND FREE", with the vignettes recording the country's progress "in the development of her resources in the happiness of her people from Poverty, Misery and Anarchy",[25]' and yet the tone of the novel rapidly sinks into gloom and pessimism. Lever himself admitted that 'the whole company which he called together to be pleasant turned out little better than a party of undertakers'.[26] Sutherland suggests that this negativity was the result of the novelist's growing concern over the book's failure with the reading public. While his anxiety almost certainly influenced the novel's atmosphere, there is, in fact, even in the earliest stages, very little evidence that its subject would allow much room for optimism. Admittedly, the Knight's story ends on a positive note: through the efforts of his friend, Bagenal Daly, the villainy of the Hickmans in sponsoring Gleeson's criminal activities is eventually revealed, and he is restored to his own. This optimism cannot, however, be transposed to the wider political picture. In the half century between the Union and the writing of *The Knight of Gwynne*, there had been precious little evidence that Ireland would enjoy a restoration of its political independence, as symbolized by its own parliament. Furthermore, like so many other Irish

An Iniquitous Act

Protestants, Lever believed that such a restoration would now only exacerbate Ireland's problems, and that a restored parliament would be as likely as its British counterpart to distort Irish views. Because of its incorporation of such serious and gloomy concerns, Lionel Stevenson, like Sutherland, identified *The Knight of Gwynne* as a vital watershed in Lever's career:

> This serious and articulate purpose is utterly unlike the jaunty extemporizing, interspersed with irresolution, by which his earlier novels were composed. His education as a novelist had been unusually protracted, but it was now complete. The obstinate romanticism . . . was tempered at last by repeated contact with reality; the prodigal energy which had sustained him through his first four books with airy disregard of structure and coherence had flagged as he neared the bottom of his coffer of anecdotes; his fifth and sixth books had been anxious fumbling with problems of technique and social purpose . . . Of his literary maturity *St Patrick's Eve* was the first utterance and his departure from Ireland the confirmation; but the full measure of it was not revealed until *The Knight of Gwynne*.[27]

At the conclusion of his novel, Lever remained true to the vow of integrity which he had made at its commencement.[28] The immediately preceding *St Patrick's Eve* was allowed a happy ending, with the hitherto absentee landlord resuming his traditional responsibilities. Without rewriting history, or else by casting the end of his novel in an imagined future, the same happy conclusion could not be tacked onto his novel of the Union.

Mary Martin dispenses charity to the tenants of Cro' Martin. While the bare outline of Mary's career – a rightful inheritance denied, a life of selfless charity concluding with exhaustion and death – would appear to be the stock-in-trade of Victorian melodrama, her fate is rendered altogether more interesting by Lever's insistence upon her frequent wrong-headedness, upon her inability to accept political reality and upon the fact that her efforts are rendered futile by decades of landlord neglect.

4

THE DOUBLE-SIDED COIN

– I –

By the 1850s Lever had already proved that he was a serious novelist capable of handling issues of political and social importance. His readership could no longer be in any doubt that the rumbustious novels of Dr Quicksilver were a thing of the past and that he had moved on, developing both his talents and his concerns. For all his continuing claims regarding the haphazard nature of his writing, *The O'Donoghue*, *St Patrick's Eve* and *The Knight of Gwynne* had revealed his increasing preoccupation with the mature expression of deeply held convictions concerning both the condition of Ireland and its people, and the forces which had shaped them.

During this decade he showed no signs of reducing his astonishing rate of composition and added a further ten titles to his rapidly expanding list of completed novels. Of these ten, by far the most important are *The Dodd Family Abroad* and *The Martins of Cro' Martin*. Written consecutively, these novels are generally considered to be two of his finest works, evincing both maturity and confidence. Their methods of treatment are as entirely unlike as their subjects, thereby exhibiting his considerable versatility. *The Dodd Family Abroad* is his only mature essay at comedy, written in the form of epistles sent to various friends by the members of the Dodd family as they tour the Continent in search of culture and economy. The comedy is provided by their misconceptions of Europe and the Europeans and by the sequence of ridiculous adventures in which they become embroiled as they travel from town to town and from country to country. However, despite its light-hearted tone, *The Dodd Family Abroad* is a novel with a number of serious purposes. In writing it, Lever was concerned with the themes of national identity and the misconceptions of national character resulting from xenophobia and condescension. There is a thread of political commentary running through the narrative, and the prejudices of the Dodds concerning their Continental hosts find their parallel in the English government's mistaken views of Ireland and the Irish.

The veiled didacticism of *The Dodd Family Abroad* is not duplicated in *The Martins of Cro' Martin*. Whilst the first novel is an outwardly comical analysis of prejudice, the second is a gloomy survey of the tragic results of landlord irresponsibility and the consequent destruction of the traditional compact between land-owner and tenant. Through *The Dodd Family Abroad* Lever incites his readers to a better understanding of their neighbours and in *The Martins of Cro' Martin* he reveals how a lack of understanding and mutual respect can warp and destroy social structures of a thousand years' growth. Written between September 1852 and June 1856, these two very different novels, one essentially optimistic and the other pessimistic, might reasonably be considered to represent the opposing sides of their author's personality and political philosophy.

– II –

In reading Lever's comments on *The Dodd Family Abroad* it is refreshing to discover that the novelist was almost entirely satisfied with the results of his labours and, even more surprisingly, that its composition afforded him 'much pleasure'.[1] In 1863, ten years after the serial publication, he wrote to John Blackwood:

How glad I am you like *The Dodds*. I know I have never done, nor ever shall do, anything one half so good, because it is original.[2]

As with the later *Sir Brook Fossbrooke*, the novelist's opinion of his work ill-accorded with that of his audience. Although the performance elicited praise from his friends, with the reading public it failed to find favour and Lever's bitterness at its neglect found poignant expression on more than one occasion:

I never could bring myself yet, nor do I hope to arrive at the point hereafter, to respect my Public; and I often hug myself, in the not very profitable consolation, that they never thought meaner of me nor do I of them. I know that the very worst things I ever did were instant successes, and some one or two – as *The Dodds*, for instance, which had a certain stamp of originality – were total and lamentable failures.[3]

In attempting to identify the causes of the book's failure, Lionel Stevenson pointed towards its discursiveness and the use of the old-fashioned device of epistolary construction, claiming, in opposition to Lever's own belief, that the novel lacked originality.[4] Although these criticisms have a certain weight, particularly with reference to the modern audience's discomfort with the epistolary form, as a mature comedy, with a serious underlying political purpose and skilfully drawn, psychologically convincing characters, we might now fairly claim that *The Dodd Family Abroad* is one of Lever's finest works. Certainly, the modern critical reader is likely to find himself accepting Lever's own decision to accord it a position of prominence among his novels.

Fitzpatrick tells us that Lever had first considered writing an epistolary novel when he was planning *Sir Jasper Carew* (1855) but that he had abandoned the scheme because it might interfere with the development of the plot.[5] With *The Dodd Family Abroad*, however, his anxieties were overcome and he confidently asserted that 'each character is so contrived as to evoke, in the most humorous form, the peculiarities of all the others, without any violation of the individuality assigned to itself'.[6] Without doubt, the novel contains some of his best drawn characters and its epistolary form rather aids than curbs their development.

In his references to *The Dodd Family Abroad* Lever frequently dwells on Kenny, head of the Dodd family, clearly believing him to be one of his best-drawn Irishmen:

I decanted, through all the absurdities of Dodd's nature, whatever I really knew of life and mankind, and it is that very admixture of shrewd sense and intense blundering that makes an Irishman. The perception and the enjoyment of the very domestic absurdities that overwhelm him with shame would in any other nature mean insanity, but they only make an Irishman very true to his national characteristics, and rather a pleasant fellow to talk to.[7]

There is evidence that the idea of creating a comic fiction from a touring family's ignorance of European manners and society had occurred to Lever long before he began *The Dodd Family Abroad*. His early series of essays, *Nuts and Nutcrackers* and *Tales of the Trains*, both contain references to trans-Channel misunderstandings and, in the latter work, the essay 'Mr Blake in Belgium' contains a character bearing a very close resemblance to Kenny Dodd. Not only are they both hen-pecked and plethoric, but their motivations for sampling life on the Continent are nearly identical:

'I was persuaded by my wife that we ought to go and live abroad for economy – that there would be no end to the saving we'd make by leaving our house in Galway, and taking up our residence in France or Belgium. First we'd let the place for at least six hundred a year... then we'd send away all the lazy "old hangers-on," as my wife called them, such as the gatekeepers, and gardeners, and stable-boys. These, her sister told her, were "eating us up" entirely... She told my wife that Ireland was the lowest place of all; nobody would think of bringing up their family there; no education, no manners, and worst of all, no men that could afford to marry.'[8]

Kenny's letters make up the bulk of the novel and though Lever expressed his wish to make all of the characters 'marked and distinguished',[9] it was in the detailed portrayal of his plump, irascible and home-sick hero that his efforts found their centre. In his assessment of the novel, Stevenson has described its premiss as 'purely farcical and not a little hackneyed' and its characters as 'stock figures';[10] but such a summary does not do justice to the skill with which Lever delineates each of his creations, Kenny above all. That Kenny held an important position in the novelist's heart there can be no doubt:

I felt an amount of interest in the character of Kenny Dodd such as I have never felt before nor since experienced for any personage of my own creation.[11]

Tony Bareham's analysis of the portrait's success is very much at variance with Stevenson's; he describes Kenny as 'an original comic masterpiece. Eccentric, explosive, pungent'.[12] Indeed, Kenny's individuality grows to an astonishing degree and as the pressures bearing upon him increase – legal, financial and domestic – he soon commands the reader's entire sympathy. The full extent of our empathy is nowhere more apparent than in the sequence of episodes in which the hen-pecked hero is duped by the beautiful and beguiling Mrs Gore Hampton and her accomplice Lord George Tiverton. In describing the family's growing intimacy with the adventuress, Kenny explains how Continental life and manners have eroded their normal social reserve and caution, thereby highlighting the novel's predominant concern with the British tourists' 'preconceived ideas of a certain latitude in morals' and their resolve 'to have the benefit of it':[13]

It may sound strange that we should have formed so close alliance while in ignorance of these circumstances, and, doubtless, in our own country, the inquiry would have preceded the ratification of this compact, but the habits of the Continent, my dear Tom, teach very different lessons. All social transactions are carried on upon principles of unlimited credit, and you endorse every bill of passing acquaintanceship with a most reckless disregard to the day of presentation for payment.[14]

While he is able to dissect the effects of their European lifestyle, Kenny fails to learn by his mistakes; he looks before he leaps, but leaps nevertheless. Having resisted the charms and denied the benefits of life away from Ireland, as they are expounded by his wife and children, it is the enchantment of Mrs Gore Hampton and Kenny's susceptibility to her beauty and graces which persuade him of his mistake:

> When the Continent was closed to us by the war, there was a home stamp upon all our manufactures – our chairs and tables, our knives and our candlesticks, were all made after native models, solid and substantial enough, but, I believe, neither very artistic nor graceful. We were used to them, however, and as we had never seen any other, we thought them the very perfection of their kind. The Peace of '15 opened our eyes, and we discovered, to our infinite chagrin and astonishment, that, in matters of elegance and taste, we were little better than barbarians . . .
> I'll tell you where we felt this discrepancy most remarkably – in our women, Tom. . . .[15]

In retrospect, Kenny is able to identify his own motivations and the progress of Mrs Gore Hampton's influence, but he remains susceptible to it. It is this combination of self-knowledge and acknowledged weakness, of 'shrewd sense and intense blundering', which make Kenny so endearing to the reader. Stevenson identifies the deliberately constructed dissonance in his character as one of the chief flaws in the novel, but many readers will consider it to be one of the strengths of the portrait, and as we witness the tightening of the tricksters' web we feel an almost painful sympathy for Kenny's plight. In so powerfully engaging our sympathy for a comic character, Lever again exhibits his brilliance as a creator and observer of human character.

More than ten years after the completion of *Harry Lorrequer* and *Charles O'Malley*, Lever revealed in *The Dodd Family Abroad* that he had lost none of his ability to create comedy of a type which might be appreciated by the early admirers who had subsequently become disenchanted by his growing seriousness. Kenny is the hero of many adventures which are quite ludicrous, for instance when, at the head of a party of artisans with whom he has been travelling, and witnessed by his son James, he breaks up an extravagantly expensive picnic arranged by his wife:

> bounding over the table with a formidable old tongues in my hand, I reached the door just as it gave way to the assaulting party, and came flat down off the hinges, discovering the forlorn hope of the enemy led on by – oh, shame and disgrace ineffable! – no other than my father himself! There he was, Bob, without his coat, with a large saucepan in one hand for a shield, and a kitchen cleaver in the other. He vociferously cheered on his followers to the breach. . . .
> I have often heard that no description can convey even the faintest notion of the horrors of a town taken by assault. I now believed it.[16]

Such a scene might justly be compared with the finest comedy in the early novels, but despite his conspicuous role in this and similar episodes, Kenny is never reduced to the diminished stature of a mere clown, and it is in the fact that he is clearly intelligent that we can discover the root of his hold upon our emotions. While creating such boisterous mayhem, Lever's maturity both as man and artist enabled him to utilise subtle characterisation to immense effect within the framework of the novel. It is, indeed, the psychological realism of the characterisation which lends the comedy its piquancy and remains one of the work's outstanding merits.

– III –

In referring to *The Dodd Family Abroad*, Lever described Kenny as 'the *cheval de bataille* of the performance' and expressed his hope that through him he would be able to 'make the whole readable'.[17] That the novel in general, and Kenny in particular, were intended to serve a dual purpose Lever never denied, and, in writing to his friend Alexander Spencer, he declared that 'through all its absurdity of incident and situation I have endeavoured to convey whatever I know of life and the world'.[18] However, though he uses his hero as the mouthpiece for many of his own thoughts on the condition of Ireland and Europe, Lever never allows Kenny to become a mere cipher:

I by no means intend to endorse as my own every judgement of K.J., but I mean that many of his remarks are, so far as I am capable of saying, just and correct, and when he does blunder, it is only for the sake of preserving that species of characteristic which should take off any appearance of dogmatism or pretension when speaking of more important subjects.[19]

By 1853 it had become impossible that Lever should ever revert to the artlessness and political naiveté of his early career. Though it was usually astutely veiled, and given expression almost exclusively through the realistic dialogue of his characters, his artistic motivation had become increasingly didactic. This motivation is no less present in the comical *The Dodd Family Abroad* than in the avowedly serious *The O'Donoghue* or in the overtly tragic *The Martins of Cro' Martin*. Running through the series of ludicrous incidents, fuelled as they are by error and misconception, there is an unbroken thread of political comment on the condition of Ireland and on English misrule. It was possibly this portion of the novel's content which found the least favour with Lever's English readers, who may have considered themselves duped into reading a political homily by the novel's ostensible guise of picaresque comedy.

The Double-Sided Coin

In his 1872 preface to *Harry Lorrequer*, Lever admitted that in creating his rakish young hero he had drawn upon his own character, and there can be little doubt that he resorted to the same process when portraying the middle-aged Kenny Dodd. Certainly we might feel confident in identifying many of the fictional character's opinions concerning Ireland with those of the author. Both are essentially Tory in their outlook, but both are clear-sighted in their criticisms of English policy towards Ireland. In Letter Nine, for instance, Kenny gives his unmistakably Leverian view of the English press:

the *Times* is too fond of blackguarding us. What's the use of it? What good does it ever do? I may throw mud at a man every day till the end of the world, but I'll never make his face the cleaner for it![20]

The expression of views upon the condition of Ireland begins almost immediately and continues throughout the novel's length, thereby revealing Lever's inability to completely disassociate himself from the increasingly political nature of his motivation as an artist. Although the politicisation of his comedy may have dismayed his readers, the agenda which he followed resulted in his making a number of deeply sincere statements. Kenny's emotional outcry at the continuing depopulation of Ireland, for instance, must rank as one of Lever's most potent and impassioned expressions of his own Nationalist feelings:

There is a stir and a movement going forward, it is true; but unlike that which betokens the march of prosperity and gain, it only implies transition. Ay, Tom, all is changing around us. The Gentry are going, the Middle Classes are going, and the Peasant is going; some, of their free will; more, from necessity. I know that the general opinion is favourable to all this – in England at least. The cry is ever, 'Ireland is improving – Ireland will be better.' But my notion is, that by Ireland we should understand not alone the soil, the rocks, and the rivers, but the people – the heart, and soul, and life-blood that made the island the generous, warm-hearted, social spot that we once knew it. Take away these, and I no longer recognise it as my country. What matters it to me if the Scotchman or the Norfolk farmer is to prosper where we only could exist? My sympathies are not with him. You might as well try and console me for the death of my child by showing me how comfortably some other man's boy could sleep in his bed.[21]

To the modern reader the intrusion of such political opinions into an otherwise comical novel might appear somewhat clumsy, and Stevenson identifies this seeming inconsistency as the main reason for the book's falling 'rather flat with readers looking for a sequential tale straightforwardly told',[22] but the duality of *The Dodd Family Abroad* might certainly be cited by Lever's defenders against the still prevalent Nationalist accusations of social and political irresponsibility.

– IV –

Whether his subject be misrule in Ireland or the prevalent British misconceptions of European life, throughout *The Dodd Family Abroad* Lever was writing from personal experience and it is this reliance upon what he had himself observed that constitutes one of the novel's greatest strengths. For instance, he was a life-long devotee to whist, and in *The Dodd Family Abroad* we find one of his most powerful depictions of the thrill of gaming:

> I do not speak here of the terrible infatuation of play, and the almost utter impossibility of resisting it, but I allude to what is infinitely worse, the certainty of your applying play theories and play tactics to every event and circumstance of real life.
>
> The whole world becomes to you but one great green cloth, and everything in it a question of Luck! Will the bad run continue here? Will good fortune stand much longer to you? You grow to regard yourself as utterly powerless and impassive; a football at the toe of destiny![23]

We know from Fitzpatrick that Lever had an intimate familiarity with his subject, that he had played at Baden in 1848, and that he had lost so heavily that he was obliged to write two novels simultaneously: *Con Cregan* and *The Daltons* .[24] By translating his first-hand experiences into art, he provides us with a brilliant analysis of the almost hypnotic fascination of gambling.

In another aspect of *The Dodd Family Abroad* his dependence on his own observations becomes particularly significant. It is as a European novel that the work merits further detailed consideration. In 1939, on the eve of World War II, Lionel Stevenson pointedly claimed that the novel had an undeniable relevance for the contemporary audience:

> It contains many remarks upon the national characteristics and political ambitions of Germany, Italy and other countries, that are astonishingly applicable today.[25]

By the time of writing *The Dodd Family Abroad* Lever had been resident on the Continent for the best part of a decade, having lived in Belgium, Germany, Austria and Italy. His intimate familiarity with Europe almost certainly exceeded that of any other British novelist of his generation and he attempted to utilise his knowledge for serious ends. Within the context of his times it is understandable that Stevenson should attempt to claim that Lever was primarily concerned with alerting his lethargic English audience to the 'political ambitions' of the European powers, though, in the light of this interpretation, it is ironic that Lever should claim that it was the Germans who best understood the message of his novel.[26] In reality, his main concern was with highlight-

The Double-Sided Coin

ing the misinterpretations and mistakes to which prejudice and lack of familiarity could give rise on both sides of the English Channel:

> As to the [? criticism] about foreigners and the Continent generally, I assure you I have not the courage to tell the things that have come under my own notice, while foreign notions of England are equally, if not more, ridiculous.[27]

In a period in which the debate over the future of Europe fills our newspapers daily, *The Dodd Family Abroad* has a very real relevance. The swiftness of television and the other media would seem to have done little to correct many of our misconceptions; and as an Irishman, a Briton, and a European, Lever's perception of our rooted prejudices has a particular pertinence.

– V –

As *The Knight of Gwynne* had been designed as an examination of the causes and effects of the 1800 Act of Union, *The Martins of Cro' Martin* was Lever's commentary on the ramifications of the 1829 Catholic Emancipation, or Relief, Act. In choosing for his subject matter the growing antagonism between the landholding, predominantly Protestant aristocracy and the Catholic peasantry and growing middle-classes, he created a novel of conflict. But the conflict is not limited to the protagonists of the fiction; indeed, it represents Lever's sincere attempt to identify and reconcile his traditional Tory sympathies and the increasingly radical political realism resulting from his mature experience and observation.

The novel is almost invariably linked with the earlier *St Patrick's Eve*, primarily because, in writing the two books, Lever called upon his experiences as a young cholera doctor, and because in both works he concerns himself with the traditional feudal relationship between the peasants and their landlords. However, in its treatment of these subjects *The Martins of Cro' Martin*, which has been called Lever's *Bleak House* by Tony Bareham,[28] constitutes a very considerable advance in Lever's career. Intended as an admonition to the landlords who had deserted their estates after the Act of Union, *St Patrick's Eve*, in essence, is a romanticised view of the bond which should exist between land-owner and tenant, the one offering protection, the other reciprocating with fidelity in an idealised expansion of the father-son relationship. By the end of the short novel, the landlord has returned to his seat, wrongs have been righted and there is a sense of optimism. That in 1845 Lever believed in the validity of this time-honoured contract, and the possibility of such a happy ending through the acknowledgment of responsibility, there can be not a shadow of a doubt; but by the early 1850s, whilst still having faith in the ideal, he had come to accept that the period when such a relationship could be maintained or, rather, re-instituted, had passed for good. This realisation was a bitter one, and through *The Martins of Cro' Martin* Lever worked out his response to it.

The heroine of the novel is Mary Martin, daughter of a prodigal younger son and niece to the current landlord Godfrey Martin. In Mary we are presented with the ideal of the responsible land-owner: she accepts her position of affluence as one of responsibility to the tenantry:

> She might have made many a mistake in the characters of those for whom she was interested – conceived many a false hope – nurtured many a delusive expectation; but in the scheme of life she had planned out for herself, the exalting sense of a duty more than recompensed her for every failure.[29]

With her energy, enthusiasm and genuine love of the people, Mary has accepted the management of the estate, and her activity is in sharp contrast with the indolent and effete lifestyle of Godfrey Martin whose one concern is with his own uninterrupted ease. In his earliest fiction Lever portrayed the ruinous and irresponsible existence of the Irish squirearchy with humour and indulgence. Godfrey Martin is a later development of Godfrey O'Malley, but Lever's depiction of Martin exhibits none of the sympathy which he clearly felt for his earlier creation – his youthful love of the racy self-indulgence of the rack-renting squire has been replaced by a sincere abhorrence of the results of such an existence on the landlord's dependent tenants. Our sympathies are immediately engaged for Mary, whose self-denial and conscientious devotion to duty are very much at variance with Martin's selfishness. Although he can never summon the energy to conquer his apathy, Martin is shown to have a genuine love of his estate and of the people; however, neither his wife, Lady Dorothea, nor his son and heir, Captain Harry Martin, share this love. Lady Dorothea views the peasantry as little other than a drain on the resources of the estate, and in her passionate reaction to Mary's schemes for their employment and support, reveals both her complete ignorance of their circumstances and her immunity to any feelings of proprietorial responsibility:

> 'Employs the people! How I hate that cant phrase! Can't they employ themselves on their own farms? Haven't they digging and draining, and whatever it is, to do of their own? Must they of necessity depend on us for support, and require that we should institute useless works to employ them?'[30]

Lady Dorothea's harshness and ignorance, however, are perhaps not

Lever's portrait, as drawn by Samuel Lover (1797-1868) and engraved by Phiz. The portrait was taken while Lever was resident in Brussels and served as frontispiece to the first edition of *Jack Hinton* (1843). The novelist was reluctant to have his portrait published, and requested that, 'if given at all, put me in a quiet vignette, and mounted on a cob'.

Templeogue House, Dublin, photographed towards the end of the nineteenth century (above) and as it appears today (below). Lever lived here while he edited the *Dublin University Magazine* (1842-1845). Originally a foundation of the Knights Templar, the house was remodelled during the seventeenth, eighteenth and nineteenth centuries – though each building incorporated elements of the original castle, which proved too strong for demolition. Its incorporation of various architectural styles may well have inspired such fictional houses as O'Donoghue Castle and Kilgobbin Castle, though its most precise fictional counterpart is, perhaps, the house of the corrupted land agent 'Honest Tom' Gleeson in *The Knight of Gwynne*. Traditionally Lever is said to have written his novels during this period in a tower room of the ancient castle.

The profound change in Lever's choice and treatment of subject might, in part at least, be attributed to the criticisms of William Carleton (1794-1869). Carleton's peasant upbringing and Nationalist sympathies made him in many ways the antithesis of the well-born and Tory Anglo-Irish novelist but they shared a strong desire to portray elements of Irish society accurately and without prejudice, though the elements which each chose were at the opposite ends of the social spectrum.

The novelist George Whyte-Melville (1821-78), who served as a major of Turkish irregular cavalry during the Crimean War. Though many of his works are meritorious, the only novel in which he called upon his Crimean experiences, *The Interpreter* (1858), is one of his weakest. It reveals an apparent unwillingness to engage with and expand upon his first-hand knowledge of the conflict. The same reluctance can be identified in at least some of the works of Lever's mentor, the Waterloo veteran, W. H. Maxwell. In contrast with such soldiers-turned-authors, Lever perhaps benefited from not having seen the harsh reality of warfare and was able to produce thrilling and imaginative descriptions of battle. Yet his attention to detail was so precise that many veterans believed that he must be of their number.

The military and sporting novelist, William Hamilton Maxwell (1792-1850). After military service during the Peninsular Campaigns and at Waterloo, Maxwell became a clergyman and was incumbent of Ballagh in Connemara. Lever refers to his friendship with Maxwell in his 1872 preface to *Harry Lorrequer* and there can be no doubt that the latter's descriptions of military life in such works as *Stories of Waterloo* (1834) and *Stories of the Peninsular War* (1837), exerted a profound influence on Lever's early writing career. Maxwell subsequently moved to Scotland where he died in obscurity. He is buried in Musselburgh, on the outskirts of Edinburgh.

In 1874, Lever's daughter, Mrs Nevill, presented his writing chair and table to his Alma Mater, Trinity College, Dublin. He almost certainly used this chair when writing his masterpiece, *Lord Kilgobbin*. Unfortunately, the location of the table is now unknown, though the chair continues to reside in the Librarian's office.

While Lever was always – and often adversely – influenced by the demands of his publishers, none, perhaps, enjoyed his respect to the degree of John Blackwood (1818-1879). Blackwood published three of Lever's novels – *A Rent in a Cloud* (1865), *Tony Butler* (1865) and *Sir Brook Fossbrooke* (1866) – as well as the *Cornelius O'Dowd* essays between 1864 and 1872. The canny Scots publisher was particularly adept at handling the novelist, who often veered between diffidence and touchiness, and the two remained firm friends until the latter's death.

Lever aged about forty, drawn by the English artist Stephen Pearce, probably at Bagni di Lucca. Pearce first met Lever at Templeogue in 1844 and the two appear to have formed an almost instant friendship. Acting as the novelist's amanuensis and travelling companion, Pearce stayed with the Levers for two years, finally leaving them after they took up residence at the Rieder Schloss in the Tyrol. It was here that *The Knight of Gwynne* was written.

quite as revolting as the sentiments expressed by her spendthrift son, when the starving and diseased condition of the tenants is made known to him:

> 'Mary here coolly asks you, in the spirit of this same improvement-scheme, to relinquish a year's income, and make a present of I know not how much more, simply because things are going badly with them, just as if everybody hasn't their turn of ill-fortune. Egad, I can answer for it, mine hasn't been flourishing latterly, and yet I have heard of no benevolent plan on foot to aid or release me!'[31]

In his heartless vacuity Harry Martin is actually capable of comparing his own self-imposed lack of funds to the destitution of the people for whom, one day, he must accept responsibility. Lever's condemnation of such an attitude is explicit, and yet Harry Martin in his extravagance and recklessness is not really so very far removed from the Harry Lorrequers and Charles O'Malleys of the early novels.

That the Martins have become divorced from their traditional place within the social hierarchy is made clear from the very earliest stage of the novel. From being an essential component in the traditional system of mutual support and maintenance they are now seen as an essentially alien graft on the landscape. Nowhere is this made more explicit than in Lever's early descriptions of the Cro' Martin estate. Tony Bareham has described this process:

> we pan in on Cro' Martin Castle, cut off by high walls and gates from its surroundings. The castle exerts some influence over local geography; there are plantations, evidence of cultivation in the environs. But Lever sweeps onwards to an interior description, as though to point up the world of the have-nots in the bleak outdoors, and the haves within the walled sanctuary of the castle.[32]

Bareham then goes on to consider the symbolism of the house's furnishings and to quote from the novel itself:

> The spotless windows of plate-glass, the polished floor that mirrored every chair that stood on it, the massive and well-fitting doors, the richly gilded dogs that shone within the marble hearth, had little brotherhood with the dreary dwellings of the cottiers beyond the walls of the park – and certainly even Irish misery never was more conspicuous than in that lonely region.[33]

For all the hardship of their existence, the peasants are, in fact, more at one with their environment. Despite the centuries of their proprietorship, the Martins are portrayed as interlopers. Once beyond the rarefied atmosphere of the castle itself, they are on foreign territory, indifferent to the beauties of the landscape and uncomfortable in the climate. Only Mary, who rides on horseback or in an open pony-carriage, seems to be at home amidst the landscape and the elements, indeed, the rest of the Martins are practically never seen outside at all.

– VI –

Although Mary's motivation and ideals are seen to be the models upon which the management of the great estates should have been founded, the predominantly pessimistic tone of the novel reveals that Lever could not deny to himself, or to his readers, his conviction that the time for a reversion to such practices had passed. By decades of rackrenting and ruinous expenditure the landlord class had forfeited its traditional role within the community, and the attempts of any individual, no matter how highly principled, to reinvigorate the class and to acknowledge its responsibilities could only be seen, politically, as the last throes of an outmoded institution.

Through his description of the barrister Valentine Repton, Lever expresses his regret for the loss of the rich and cosmopolitan life for which Dublin was renowned before the Act of Union:

> The presence of a Parliament in Ireland imparted a dignity and importance to society, while it secured to social intercourse the men who made that Senate illustrious. The Bar, too, of former days was essentially the career of the highest class ... and thus the wit, the brilliancy, and the readiness which gives conversation its charm, obtained the high culture which comes of a learned profession, and the social intercourse with men of refined understanding.
> With the Union this spirit died out.[34]

This nostalgia, this wistfulness, applies also to Lever's view of the landholding classes, though it does not negate his painful recognition of their present redundancy. He chooses Repton, the representative of another dying breed, to identify the irremediable decline of the Martins and their kind:

> 'It is too late to try the feudal system in the year of our Lord 1829, Miss Martin. We live in an age where everything is to be redressed by a Parliament. The old social compact between proprietor and peasant is repealed, and all must be done by "the House." Now, if your grandfather had pursued the path that you are doing today, this crisis might never have arrived; but he did not, young lady. He lived like a real gentleman; he hunted, and drank, and feasted, and rack-rented, and horsewhipped all around him.'[35]

Nobly-intentioned as they are, Mary's schemes for the improvement of the estate and for the aid of the peasantry, cannot halt the inevitable. The traditional social contract, the landlord's side of which unwritten bargain Mary is trying to fulfil, has been rendered obsolete by political developments. Furthermore, by failing to formulate a political strategy, as opposed to a purely social one, Mary exhibits her naiveté and condemns her own efforts to ultimate defeat:

> 'If you mean, by the country, the lives and fortunes of those who live in it – the people by whose toil it is fertilised – by whose traits it is a nation – I tell you frankly that I yield to none for interest in all that touches them; but if you come to talk of privileges and legislative benefits, I know nothing of them; they form a land of whose geography I am ignorant.'[36]

Without political intent, Mary's championship of the peasantry and of Irish national identity can produce no long term benefits. In denying her a political motivation, Lever does not justify her position by pointing out that, as a woman, she can have no political career. Instead, and contrary to what one might expect of a novelist who took almost every possible opportunity to reveal the restrictions of a male-dominated society, he attributes Mary's a-political stance to personal choice or lack of aptitude.

Her lack of political motivation is in stark contrast with the impulses of the novel's secondary heroine, Kate Henderson, the foster-daughter of the Martins' agent. In the strength of her political beliefs and in her influence over the male characters of the novel, Kate is perhaps more typical of other Leverian heroines such as Kate O'Donoghue and Nina Kostalergi. Her sympathies are essentially republican and meritocratic. Her reaction to Mary's plea for financial aid for the peasants is as uncompromising as that of Lady Dorothea, though of a very different nature:

> 'to say that now is the time to show these poor people the saving care and protection that the rich owe them, as if the duty dated from the hour of their being struck down by famine – laid low by pestilence! or that the debt could ever be acquitted by the relief accorded to pauperism! Why not have taught these same famished creatures self-dependence, elevated them to the rank of civilised beings by the enjoyment of rights that give men self-esteem as well as liberty?'[37]

Having lost their parliamentary seat through the Catholic voters' newly obtained ability to elect an individual who will represent their own views, the Martins desert their estate in disgust. They travel to Paris, where they arrive just in time for the 1830 revolution and the deposition of Charles X. Rather unconvincingly Kate is discovered to be a prime-mover among the revolutionaries, and her political theories find physical expression. Stevenson has accurately stated that in his depiction of the revolution Lever's sympathies are 'distinctly proletarian'.[38] In his description of the arrogance and luxurious self-indulgence of the French royalists we might discover a parallel with the lifestyle and attitudes of Ascendancy families such as the Martins:

To have heard the sentiments then uttered, the disparaging opinions expressed of the middle and humbler classes, the hopelessness of ever seeing them sufficiently impressed with their own inferiority, the adulation bestowed on the monarch and all around him, one might really have fancied himself back again at the Tuileries in the time of Louis the Fourteenth.[39]

The revolution, led largely by the middle-classes, sweeps away the gilded courtiers and their pretensions in a matter of seventy-two hours, and the message which Lever conveys is that a similar event might easily see the end of the irresponsible and feckless Irish squirearchy. The transfer to Paris of many of the novel's leading protagonists becomes, through the description of the revolution, not an unnecessary digression but a pointed and deliberate warning.

The failure of the revolutionaries to establish a new French republic and their decision to instead offer the throne to Louis-Philippe, leaves Kate Henderson disillusioned and embittered. In her political ambitions Kate has failed, as, in Ireland, Mary's social objectives meet with eventual defeat. Only in allowing Kate to acknowledge the superiority of Mary's motivation and goals does Lever indicate the object of his sympathies, but Kate's conversion, given her previous conviction, seems rather hollow; revealing one of the few occasions upon which Lever was willing to allow his wistfulness to usurp the authority of psychological realism.[40]

– VII –

Contemporary opinion concerning *The Martins of Cro' Martin* was divided. Fitzpatrick tells us that the *Athenaeum* believed Lever to have 'committed his one dull novel',[41] while the disagreement among the writer's friends caused him to remark 'everybody advises me differently – the only concurrence is when they believe me wrong, and not ever likely to be right'.[42] More recent critical reaction has tended to unite in declaring the book to be one of Lever's best, with the opinion expressed by Stevenson in 1939 being adopted by most subsequent readers:

Artistically, the book was among his highest achievements: the attitude was tolerant, the characterisation was admirably realistic, the elements of tragedy were introduced without sentimentality.[43]

This analysis correctly identifies the novel's chief merits but it fails to notice those defects which the modern reader is likely to discover, and is therefore rather unbalanced. As has been remarked already, *The Martins of Cro' Martin* is almost always identified with *St Patrick's Eve* because of the presence of cholera in both novels. Although the earlier fiction can be criticised for a sentimentality which is nowhere present in the later work, this criticism cannot be applied to the depictions of the cholera epidemic. In fact, in the short novel Lever uses his own familiarity with the ravages of the disease to far greater dramatic effect than he does in *The Martins of Cro' Martin*: the reader is introduced to the pestilence-ridden hovels of the peasantry and is spared none of the horrors which were to be found in such dwellings. The same cannot be said of the later, and larger, novel:

> On a low settle in one corner lay the figure of a young woman, whose pale, pinched features contrasted strongly with the bright ribbons of her cap floating loosely at either side. Mary tottered as she drew nigher; a terrible sense of fear was upon her – a terror of she knew not what. She held the flickering flame closer, and saw that she was dead! Poor Margaret, she had been one of Mary's chief favourites; the very cap that decked her cold forehead was Mary's wedding-gift to her.[44]

The emphasis here is on Mary's reaction to suffering and death, rather than on the physical and mental effects of cholera on its victims. In the work of the mature novelist there is an undeniable distancing from his early experiences. The reader is left in no doubt as to the devastating impact of the disease on the community: the high mortality rate, the resulting destitution and the desperate resort to emigration, but he is not shown the actual face of disease with the brusqueness for which *St Patrick's Eve* is so remarkable.

St Patrick's Eve also scores more highly in that Lever proved himself willing to attempt a detailed portrayal of the peasants as individuals, although their depiction as a social group in *The Martins of Cro' Martin* is perhaps more convincing overall. One of the primary functions of the later novel is to reveal the growing causes of division between the landlords and their tenants. However, although Lever provides us with a highly critical and searching analysis of the former, the latter remain very much on the periphery of the narrative action, in fact only one peasant character, Joan Landy, approaches to anything like individuality. The rest of the peasants are taken *en bloc*.

If we accept the limitations which Lever imposes on his description of the peasantry, then we can also admit that his general depiction has considerable merit. Take, for instance, his portrait of the women who attend Mary's levee on the lawns of Cro' Martin at the beginning of the novel:

> The expediency of misery had begotten the expediency of morals, and in all the turnings and windings of their shifty natures you could see the suggestions of that abject destitution which had eaten into their very hearts. It would have puzzled a

moralist to analyse these 'gnarled natures,' wherein some of the best and some of the worst features of humanity warred and struggled together. Who could dare to call them kind-hearted or malevolent, grateful or ungrateful, free-giving or covetous, faithful or capricious, as a people? Why, they were all of these, and fifty other things just as opposite besides, every twenty-four hours of their lives! Their moods of mind ranged from one extreme to the other; nothing had any permanency amongst them but their wretchedness.[45]

There is no sentimentality in this group portrait, neither is there any condescension or stage-Irishness. Lever portrays a people who are destitute, driven to the last extremity by a misery and want for which their landlords are largely responsible. The peasants are seen only in the company of Mary Martin, and it is clear that Lever is primarily concerned with the relationship which subsists between them. This relationship is carefully observed and psychologically convincing, from the peasants' willingness to dupe Mary where the opportunity exists, to Mary's own fear that the departure of her uncle will reduce her own status in the eyes of the tenants and, concomitantly, her ability to do good.[46]

A distinct strength in the novel is Lever's portrayal of the rising class of Catholic Irishmen whose prospects had been enriched by the Emancipation Act. At one time he may have submitted to the temptation to utilise such figures for purely comical purposes and in the earlier portions of the novel there are indications that such a temptation still existed. But as the narrative progresses he exhibits an increasing respect for such characters. By the time of writing *The Martins of Cro' Martin*, he could not contemplate a simplistic and sympathetic portrait of the landlord class, nor could he, despite his antipathy to Daniel O'Connell, satisfy his own political and artistic integrity by dismissing the reformer's supporters as comical and pretentious *petit-bourgeoisie*. One of the very few examples of comedy in the novel is provided by Mrs Nelligan's confused notions of social hierarchy:

'My mother was a Moore of Crockbawn, and her family never looked at her for marrying my father . . .

'It's true what I'm telling you. She often said it to me herself, and told me what a blessing it was, through all her troubles and trials in life – and she had her share of them, for my father was often in drink, and very cruel at times – "it supports me," she used to say, "to remember who I am, and the stock I came from, and to know that there's not one belonging to me would speak to me, nor look at the same side of the road with me, after what I done".'[47]

As a rule, however, Lever treats her class with an increasing seriousness and respect. When, for instance, an opportunity arises for the kind of drunken dinner party which would have delighted him in his early years, he exercises considerable restraint and withdraws decorously from the temptation.[48] Old Dan Nelligan, first introduced as a grasping and hard-bargaining businessman and money-lender,[49] has by the end of the novel been transformed into an essentially respectable and wholly sympathetic magistrate. The transformation is a gradual one, but it is not demanded by the constraints of the plot and instead reflects that Lever's attitudes were developing even as he wrote. From exactly the same class, and even more sympathetic, is Dan's son, Joe, whose sensitivity as a human being and brilliance as a scholar make him thoroughly deserving of the bright prospects opened to him by the Emancipation Act. Indeed, of the young men in the novel, the young and aspiring Catholic bourgeois commands our sympathies to a degree far beyond that of the two Ascendancy Protestants, the cynical and manipulative Jack Massingbred and the foppish and cold-hearted Captain Martin.

Although *The Martins of Cro' Martin* has achieved a wide acceptance as one of Lever's very best novels, it is also one of his most difficult – and the root cause of the difficulty is to be found in the fluid condition of the author's sympathies. Written as a valediction to the traditional social compact which bound peasant and landlord together, the novel also acts as an uncompromising condemnation of proprietorial abuses. Wistful in his belief that the system could and should work, Lever also admits that the corruption of the landlords renders them unworthy of continued dominance. Furthermore, as Tony Bareham has identified, while Mary Martin's selfless devotion to the tenantry demands our sympathy, 'there are hints that her energetic estate management is often wrongheaded and destructive',[50] and a further ambiguity is thereby introduced into her relationship both with those she wishes to aid and with the readers whose admiration must become tinged with doubt as to the efficacy of her activities. This uncertainty is augmented by Lever's implicit criticism of her a-political stance. Again, his Toryism does not blind him to the inherent worth and vitality of the newly emancipated shop-keeping class and the balance gradually falls in their favour. It is considerations such as these which mean that *The Martins of Cro' Martin* can never be viewed in simplistic black-and-white terms, it remains one of Lever's most demanding, but also one of his most rewarding works of fiction.

Lever examines the pleasures and perils of gaming in many of his essays and novels. His ability to write so astutely on the subject was the result of a lifetime's devotion to gambling in general, and to whist in particular. His decision to take up the pen was spurred not least by the need to supplement his income, much encroached upon by gambling debts incurred during his residence in Brussels.

5

THE ART OF BREVITY

– I –

In the few available commentaries on, and analyses of Lever's work, his numerous essays have received only the most cursory examination. This neglect is understandable since the novels merit the greatest critical attention, but he produced no fewer than five collections of essays and to ignore them completely is to pass over a volume of work to which, in his latter years particularly, he attached considerable importance and devoted much labour. The essays also provide a useful yardstick by which to measure his development both as a writer and as a man since, chronologically, they are divided between his very early and late career as a writer. Between 1845 and 1863, he devoted himself almost exclusively to writing novels, and, as we have seen, the gradual development of his style and concerns can be traced from book to book. Because of the eighteen year gap between *Nuts and Nutcrackers* and the first of the *Cornelius O'Dowd* papers, such a gradual progression cannot be observed in his career as an essayist: as readers we leap from the rather gauche and over-eager novice to the experienced man of the world, but the shock of this leap serves rather to reinforce than to obscure the span of his development.

– II –

Having assumed the editorship of the *Dublin University Magazine* in January 1842, one of Lever's first contributions in his new role was a series of papers entitled *Nuts and Nutcrackers*. Running from January 1842 to May 1844, ostensibly the series was similar in intent to Sir Thomas Browne's *Pseudoxia Epidemica* (1646): to identify commonly accepted errors and delusions in practice and belief. In the first essay, on 'Men of Genius', Lever outlines the nature of his chosen brief:

> It is a remarkable feature in the complex and difficult machinery of our society, that while crime and the law code keep steadily on the increase, moving in parallel lines one beside the other, certain prejudices, popular fallacies – nuts, as we have called them at the head of this paper – should still disgrace our social system; and that, however justice may be administered in our courts of law, in the private judicature of our own dwellings we observe an especial system of jurisprudence, marked by injustice and wrong. To endeavour to depict some instances of this, I have set about my present undertaking.[1]

Although their purposes were essentially similar, whereas Browne might be described as one of the least political writers of any age or in any language, in his own essays Lever was anxious to reveal his confidence that politics was very much his *métier*.

Fitzpatrick tells us that the series was contributed anonymously because 'its personalities, like its politics, would hit all sides; and more freedom would thereby be allowed him'.[2] Although Whigs, the Repeal Movement and its leader Daniel O'Connell were the most frequent targets for his wit and sarcasm, the Tories, with whom Lever and the *Dublin University Magazine* were traditionally allied, did not escape unscathed. Stevenson remarks that Lever was guilty of more than once 'treading unintentionally on tender corns with his jests and comments'[3] and further describes the work as 'an epitome of the outspokenness that precludes either political or editorial success'.[4] Lever's desire for anonymity, however, when coupled with his statement that he would 'endeavour to touch upon the undue estimation in which we hold certain people and places',[5] would seem to refute the argument that his disturbance of 'tender corns' was anything other than deliberate. Rather, it indicates that he was already exercising the political independence which inevitably resulted in his incurring the anger of Tory critics.[6]

Since many of the essays in *Nuts and Nutcrackers* were written in response to events reported in contemporary newspapers, to the modern reader they lack the relevance and immediacy which they possessed when first published. Their essentially ephemeral nature is revealed in the fact that, in volume form, they were published only six times between 1845 and 1899, with no subsequent edition. And yet this small book retains a certain importance in any analysis of Lever's work since the essays address a number of issues which were of abiding importance to their author. In some cases, a comparison of the youthful and mature approach to these subjects reveals a consistency of attitude; in others, a marked progression might be observed and the opinions expressed in

The Art of Brevity

this early work are found to be very much at variance with those held by the more experienced writer.

An important example of consistency can be discovered in his consideration of the prejudices resulting from the prevalent misconceptions of foreign life and manners, and in his attribution of the dissemination of such errors to the popular press:

> Once for all, then, be it known, there is no more fallacious way of forming an opinion regarding France and Frenchmen, than through the pages of our periodical press.[7]

Developing his argument, he goes on to state that 'it demands both tact and time to see that no general standard of taste can be erected for all nations' and ably illustrates the point by offering a comparison of the English and French styles of political address.[8] The subject was close to his heart, and in the later 'Nut for Foreign Travel' he inveighs against the absurd notions and deportment of those tourists who remain entirely ignorant of foreign modes and manners:

> Unsuited by their tastes – unprepared by previous information – deeming a passport and a letter of credit all-sufficient for their purpose – they set out upon their travels. From their ignorance of a foreign language, their journey is one of difficulty and embarrassment at every step. They understand little of what they see, nothing of what they hear. The discomforts of foreign life have no palliation, by their being enabled to reason on, and draw inferences from them. All the sources of information are hermetically sealed against them, and their tour has nothing to compensate for its fatigue, and expense, save the absurd detail of adventure to which their ignorance has exposed them.[9]

This description is a word-perfect epitome of *The Dodd Family Abroad*, the serialisation of which commenced some eight and a half years after the last 'nut' was published. In the novel, Lever perhaps expounds his argument more subtly, but the kernel of the philosophy which lies at the heart of *The Dodd Family Abroad* can be found in these essays. Another example of an unchanging and condemnatory reaction can be found in the essay on 'Viceregal Privileges', in which Lever unmercifully mocks the viceregal institution and, with the daring of anonymity, addresses his victims by their real names:

> every one knows that from the remotest times to the present, every viceroy of Ireland has had quite enough on his hands. Some have been saving money to pay off old mortgages, others were farming the Phoenix; some took to the King Cambyses' vein, like poor dear Lord Normanby – raked up all the old properties and faded finery of the Castle, and with such material as they could collect, made a kind of Drury-lane representation of a court.[10]

Too much can be made, however, of the supposed cowardice of attacking from behind the veil of an anonymous authorship. The editor of the *Dublin University Magazine* was responsible for all decisions relating to content, and if the remarks of a contributor were found to be objectionable then the editor was held liable for allowing publication. The onerousness of this responsibility is demonstrated in the fact that Lever came close to fighting a duel over an article which attacked the temperance campaigner, Samuel Carter Hall.[11] The pretension and hollowness of viceregal life remained one of his favourite targets throughout his writing career and, having found early expression in this 'nut,' it would continue to feature in novels such as *The O'Donoghue*, *Roland Cashel* and *Lord Kilgobbin*.

Although such mockery might offend the authorities, it would almost certainly find favour with Irishmen from a wide cross-section of political persuasions, including the Nationalists. The same could not be said of certain remarks to be found in other 'nuts' and this small volume contains some of Lever's most unsympathetic writing. The once common accusations of his supposed willingness to pander to English perceptions of Irish barbarism almost invariably make reference to *Harry Lorrequer* and *Charles O'Malley*, but nowhere in either of those novels is there a statement so likely to arouse Nationalist antipathy as the following passage from 'A Nut for Learned Societies':

> as to history, all the world knows that since the Flood the Irish have never done anything else than make love, illicit whiskey, and beat each other. What nonsense, then, to talk about the ancient cultivation of the land, of its high rank in literature, and its excellence in art. A stone bishop, with a nose like a negro, and a crosier like a garden-rake, are the only evidences of our ancestors' taste in sculpture; and some doggerel verses in Irish, explaining how King Phelim O'Toole cheated a brother monarch out of his small-clothes, are about the extent of our historic treasures.[12]

Such a negative summary of Irish culture, created in order to excite laughter, still has the power to evoke feelings of surprise and anger, and one must assume that the reaction produced in a contemporary audience cannot have been markedly dissimilar. We have already seen that Lever's sympathies underwent a continual process of refinement, and that his development was, in many ways, an extremely rapid one, and yet it remains difficult to identify the increasingly subtle and sensitive novelist with the perpetrator of such offensive solecisms. There are further examples of his apparent willingness to reinforce English convictions concerning the quaintness of the Irish, in 'A Nut for the Irish', for instance:

The Art of Brevity

But to come back to ourselves. What bold and ample views of life do our free-and-easy habits disclose to us, not to speak of the very servant at table, who will often help you to soup, when you ask for sherry, and give you preserves, when you beg for pepper. What amiable cross-purposes are we always playing at – not bigotedly adhering to our own narrow notions, and following out our own petty views of life, but eagerly doing what we have no concern in, and meritoriously performing for our friends, what they had been well pleased, we'd have let alone.[13]

The picture is not uniformly a black one. A reading of *Nuts and Nutcrackers* is certain to lend credence to the Nationalist attacks on Lever, but the volume also contains some shrewd and humorously observed comments on Ireland and on English notions regarding the Irish.

In the opening essay, Lever recounts an anecdote concerning an Irish confidence trickster named Barney Cavanagh, who 'announced some time ago that he had adopted a new system of diet, which was neither more nor less than going without food'.[14] The relation of Cavanagh's success is amusing but the most telling comment in the essay refers to the foundations for the success of this 'scam':

He was to be seen for a shilling – children half-price; and although Englishmen have read of our starving countrymen for the last century and a-half, yet their curiosity to see one, to look at him, to prod him with their umbrellas, punch him with their knuckles, and otherwise test his vitality, was such, that they seemed just as much alive as though the phenomenon was new to them.[15]

Cavanagh is taking money from his gullible English audience by exhibiting himself in the manner of a freak-show attraction, but the fact that his presentation is a voluntary one does not reduce the unpleasantness of his victims' wish to 'prod' and 'punch' him. Cavanagh is the con-man, but Lever's sympathies and, indeed, our own, lie with him and not with the bestial Englishmen; his cunning is by far preferable to their brutal stupidity. A more deliberately political analysis of events and attitudes can be found in 'A Nut for All Ireland'. In referring to Queen Victoria's recent visit to Scotland, Lever contemplates the effect upon the queen of a similar excursion to Ireland and describes the sights that will meet her eyes:

Would any charms of scenery – would any warmth of hospitality – repay her for the anguish such misery must inflict upon her, as her eye would range over the wild tract of country where want and disease seem to have fixed their dwelling, and where the only edifice that rises above the mud-cabin of the way-side presents the red brick front of a union poor-house?[16]

He emphasises the distress that the queen will experience, but the prevailing desolation and the destitution of the people leave the most lasting impression. The description is, in fact, redolent of many scenes in the later works, beginning with *The O'Donoghue* and *St Patrick's Eve*.

An important aspect of *Nuts and Nutcrackers* is Lever's willingness to address certain issues with a relative light-heartedness; and many of the issues are ones which he seriously examines in his novels. For instance, landlord absenteeism, the results of which are analysed in *St Patrick's Eve*, is humorously discussed in 'A Nut for Political Economists':

> Absenteeism is agreed on all hands to be the bane of Ireland. No one, whatever be his party prejudices, will venture to deny this. The high-principled and well-informed country gentleman professes this opinion in common with the illiterate and rabid follower of O'Connell; I need not, therefore, insist further on a proposition so universally acknowledged. To proceed – of all people, none are so naturally absentees as the Irish; in fact, it would seem that one great feature of our patriotism consists in the desire to display, in other lands, the ardent attachment we bear our own. How can we tell Frenchmen, Italians, Germans, Russians, Swedes, and Swiss, how devoted we are to the country of our birth, if we do not go abroad to do so? How can we shed tears as exiles, unless we become so?[17]

Lever carefully identifies the absentees to whom he refers: they are political exiles, the impoverished squirearchy and fortune-hunters – but there can be little doubt that he was also deliberately parodying himself: the author of Irish novels who spent so little of his adult life on his native soil. The impecunious squirearchy – a class with whom his affinity was pronounced – again receives comical treatment in 'A Nut for Younger Sons'. In this essay the heavily mortgaged landholders are presented as a possible means of subsistence:

> 'suppose, now, you have only a couple of thousand pounds to leave your son – maybe, you have not more than a single thousand – now, my advice is, not to squander your fortune in any such absurdity as a learned profession, a commission in the Line, or any other miserable existence, but just look about you, in the west of Ireland, for the fellow that has the best house, the best cellar, the best cook, and the best stable. He is sure to want money, and will be delighted to get a loan. Lend it to him: make hard terms of course. For this – as you are never to be paid – the obligation of your forbearance will be the greater. Now, mark me, from the day the deed is signed, you have snug quarters in Galway, not only in your friend's house, but among all his relations . . . you have the run of the whole concern – the best of living, great drink, and hunting in abundance. You must talk of the loan now and then, just to jog their memory; but be always "too much the gentleman" to ask for your money.'[18]

Such suggestions are remarkable for their fun: they are wry side-glances at aspects of Irish life with which Lever was intimately familiar. His comparison of the House of Lords with the Chelsea Pensioners,[19] his instituting a drunkard as an officer of the viceregal court,[20] or his relation of the tedium experienced by the intelligent man in dining out[21] cause no offence and, therefore, contrast strongly both with the discussions of subjects with which he was essentially ignorant, and with those hollow burlesque examples of stage-Irishness.

In comparison with his major novels, *Nuts and Nutcrackers* is an insignificant book. Ephemeral in nature, it contains some samples of Lever's wit which might best be forgotten, but in any analysis of his work it should be mentioned since it offers a justification, albeit a very limited one, of certain of the Nationalist criticisms which have dogged his reputation. For the same reason, it has relevance to any assessment of his development as a writer. Taken by themselves, isolated from the body of his work, these essays might reinforce the traditional condemnation of his writing but, when considered as a tiny portion of his output, the trespasses which they embody can be acknowledged as the indiscretions of a relatively inexperienced writer still uncertain of his political voice. It is inconceivable that the rapidly maturing novelist could duplicate the errors of the editorial novice.

– III –

The enthusiasm for Kenny Dodd which led Lever in his introduction to *The Dodd Family Abroad* to hint at the possibility of a sequel, *The Dodd Family in America*, also encouraged him to propose to John Blackwood the idea of a series of miscellaneous essays which he would write using Kenny Dodd as his *nom de plume*:

> It seems to me that a droll series of short papers might be well devised – Mr Kenny Dodd upon 'Men and Things in General', – a light survey taken from an Irish point of view, and consequently as often wrong as right. Next year will be a stirring one over the Continent, and afford plenty of passing events when one wanted them.[22]

Stevenson tells us that Blackwood expressed enthusiasm for the project but that he objected to the re-emergence of Kenny, a character who had first appeared in a work published by Chapman and Hall. In accepting Blackwood's reservations, Lever also revised the nature of the essays and the blunders which we might have anticipated from Kenny Dodd are dispensed with. Instead, we are presented with humorous but shrewd analysis of current events both domestic and foreign and with amusing 'jottings mainly autobiographic'.[23] Cornelius O'Dowd is, in fact, but a thinly veiled Charles Lever, and in many of the essays we can discover adventures and opinions which a reading of Fitzpatrick or Stevenson quickly enables us to identify as Lever's own.

In this reliance upon anecdote and in their conversational tone, the greatest strengths of the *Cornelius O'Dowd* essays are to be found. The voice here differs significantly from that of *Nuts and Nutcrackers*: it has less stridency and less showiness. Essentially the difference is that which is to be found between the young writer keen to make his mark in the world and the mature novelist who has become accustomed to the vicissitudes of popularity, but who retains confidence in both his gifts and his audience. As a whole the *Cornelius O'Dowd* essays are, in their attitude, far more easy-going than those written from the editorial chair of the *Dublin University Magazine*. Political references continue to abound, but there is a greater objectivity and a far greater resistance to the temptation to resort to personalities; though there is evidence that John Blackwood was at least partially responsible for this toning down.[24] 'In Retirement' was one of the last essays to be reprinted in book-form, and in it Lever describes the mood which he has wished to conjure, but the description applies as much to the early essays as to the late:

It was to talk to you that I first suggested these O'Dowderies – to have an opportunity of saying, without any thought as to the manner, or any study as to the expression, something about the scores of things which are every day turning up amongst us – to talk to you in all the freedom of intimacy, and to try if I could not infuse into our intercourse that genial sentiment that comes of a trustful freedom on one side, and a most generous and indulgent good-nature on the other.

In a word, I desired to be as much at my ease with you as though you had been sitting with me under the vine-woven trellis where I write these lines, and amid the puffs of your cuban, nodding me a kindly assent to something I have told you.[25]

A thread of wistfulness, or nostalgia runs throughout the essays. At times, indeed, we might discover an atmosphere not unlike that found in the essays of Charles Lamb, though Lever never descends to the mawkishness which occasionally mars Lamb's writing. In the essay entitled 'Glimpses of Bliss', he describes an impecunious bibliophile in a manner peculiarly reminiscent of Lamb:

I remember, when a boy, to have seen a man who passed his days wandering from one book-stall to another, stopping a while to read at each, and in this way gratifying that taste for letters his humble fortune had denied him the power of more legitimately enjoying.

He must have had some small pittance to live on, for he never seemed to do anything for his support. His dress and belongings bespoke him as very poor, and there was a degree of humility in his manner that still more indicated narrow fortune. Thus, for instance, he would never presume to occupy the place of a possible purchaser, but would move respectfully away when such approached.[26]

In another, earlier essay, 'The Decline of Whist', he handles the subject brilliantly treated by Lamb in 'Mrs Battle's Opinions on Whist'; though he offers an alternative analysis of the game rather than a continuation of his predecessor's musings. In one of innumerable references to the diplomatic corps, he describes how those trained in the subtleties of international diplomacy, in feint and counter-feint, are likely to make more accomplished whist-players than an impetuous and ardent soldier:

> It would be interesting if we had, which unhappily we have not, any statistical returns to show what classes and professions have produced the best whist-players. In my own experience I have found civilians the superiors of the military.
>
> Diplomatists I should rank first; their game was not alone finer and more subtle, but they showed a recuperative power in their play which others rarely possessed: they extricated themselves well out of difficulties, and always made their losses as small as possible.[27]

The vital words in this passage are 'in my own experience'; Lever writes from first-hand knowledge, both of the diplomatic corps and of the game itself. As a result the essay is one of his best. He goes on, in this shrewdly observed and highly amusing paper, to reveal both how an individual's method of play is a sure reflection of his behaviour and deportment away from the card-table and, indeed, how whist provides a training-ground for life.

Throughout the essays, he makes full use of observation and anecdote and, since so many of the adventures which he relates are based upon personal experience, he frequently resorts to self-dramatisation, often to very amusing effect. In the very first paper, on 'Myself', for instance, he assumes, as Cornelius O'Dowd, the identity of an impecunious Irish squire – a class with whom his sympathy is everywhere apparent – and humorously describes the process by which individuals such as himself are able to live, despite the encumbrances on their property:

> Though it is perfectly true that, what between mortgages, settlement claims, and bonds, neither my father nor myself owned these lands any more than we did the island of Jamaica, it was a great blow to me to be sold out; for, somehow or other, one can live a long time in Ireland on parchment – I mean on the mere documents of an estate that has long since passed away; but if you come once to an open sale and Judge Dobbs, there's an end of you, and you'll not get credit for a pair of shoes the day after.[28]

This is unmistakable Kenny Dodd, but it is here, despite Lever's original intentions, that Kenny ends, and Lever under the *sobriquet* O'Dowd begins. Some of the anecdotes and adventures can be definitely ascribed to actual experience, others are no doubt either fictional or based upon second-hand knowledge, but the comments upon them are essentially his own. In the second essay, on 'Adventurers', he describes a meeting with a genteel confidence-man:

> There is no quality so distinctive in this sort of man or woman – for adventurer has its feminine – as the rapid intuition with which he seizes on all available people, and throws aside all the unprofitable ones. A money-changer detecting a light napoleon is nothing to it. What are the traits by which they try humanity, I do not know, but that they do read a stranger at first sight is indisputable. That he found out Cornelius O'Dowd wasn't a member of the British Cabinet, or a junior partner in Baring's, was, you may sneeringly conjecture, no remarkable evidence of acuteness. But why should he discover the fact – fact it is – that he'd never be one penny the richer by knowing me, and that intercourse with me was about as profitable as playing a match at billiards 'for the table'?
>
> Say what people will against roguery and cheating, rail as they may at the rapacity and rascality one meets with, I declare and protest, after a good deal of experience, that the world is a very poor world to him who is not the mark of some roguery! When you are too poor to be cheated, you are too insignificant to be cherished; and the man that is not worth humbugging isn't very far from bankruptcy.
>
> It gave me a sort of shock, therefore, when I saw that my friend took this view of me, and I strolled down moodily enough to the Chamber of Deputies.[29]

By emphasising the irritation at being considered too insignificant to be the target for trickery, rather than the relief or satisfaction at escaping such an imposition, Lever makes a comic but no less realistic and shrewd comment upon the human condition, upon the importance of self-esteem and the value of inflated ideas of self-worth.

In the same essay, he acknowledges his liking for these self-same adventurers, for 'doubtful company', and admits that 'your respectable man, with a pocket-book well stored with his circular notes, and his passport in order, is as uninteresting as a "Treckshuyt" on a Dutch canal'.[30] In doing so he gives a hint as to his own artistic choices concerning character in his novels. It is a hint which he expands to great effect in the late essay, on 'The Picturesque in Morals':

> The love of the picturesque extends to ethics, all the lessons that we imbibe about order, and neatness, and symmetry, becoming vanishing views when we find ourselves in presence of fractured moralities and tottering proprieties. The incessant play of light and shade in doubtful natures makes them so pictorial to our eyes, that many a fast young lady is as good as an Etty.[31]

In comparing the pictorial fascination of the 'picturesque' with its moral counterpart, Lever provides us with a gauge both to his and our own interest in the motivations and make-up of such morally ambivalent characters as Lucy Sewell, in *Sir Brook Fossbrooke*, and to our contrasting lack of enthusiasm for the 'Edgeware Road' primness of so many Victorian heroines.[32]

The Art of Brevity

Although lightness of touch and good-nature are the hallmarks of *Cornelius O'Dowd*, as with *Nuts and Nutcrackers*, Lever finds a variety of targets for his wit and satire. In 'The English Inquisition' the all too often demeaning process of cross-examination receives the cut of his whip:

> Now, I am willing to believe that from your earliest years you have been trained to habits of virtue and order; that, good as a child, you grew better as a youth, and became best as a man; that, so circumspect had you been over your conduct through life, it would be next impossible to find an instance in which your behaviour could have been altered for the better; – in a word, that you have ever shown yourself equally zealous in the pursuit of virtue as strong in resisting every access of temptation. Get up now into the witness-box, and see what that eminent counsel will make you. Sit under him for five-and-forty minutes, and tell me if five-and-twenty years will erase the memory of the miseries you endured, the insinuations you could not reply to, the insults you were not permitted to resent?[33]

Ireland, its inhabitants, and English misrule remain favourite subjects. The Lord-Lieutenancy is mocked with no diminution of vigour, being considered 'more matter for ridicule than reverence',[34] while the low quality of Irish – and English – statuary results in the suggestion that it should be constructed from 'some perishable material'.[35] Despite such criticisms, however, there is a marked nostalgia for Ireland, heightened by a visit to Dublin in 1865. Again it is Charles Lever and not any fictional alter-ego who speaks of his enthusiasm for his home city:

> Whatever the cause, I know that I never experience the same lightness of heart, the same capacity for enjoyment, the same readiness to employ whatever faculties I possess, as in Ireland; and as I walked through the old courts of Trinity the other day, I felt a thrill through me as though thirty hard years of struggle and conflict were no more than a troubled ocean.[36]

In one of the earliest of the *Cornelius O'Dowd* essays, Lever considers the attitudes of Europe, and most particularly of Britain, to the unification movement in Italy. He then goes on to compare these attitudes to those applied to Ireland:

> I can't help thinking there are no people in Europe so much alike as the Italians and the Irish; and I ask myself, How is it that every one is so sanguine about the one, and so hopeless about the other? Why do we hear of the capacity and the intelligence of the former, and only of the latter what pertains to their ignorance and sloth? Oh! unjust generation of men! have not my poor countrymen all the qualities you extol in these same Peninsulars, plus a few others not to be disparaged?[37]

Accusations such as these, and the facility with which so many years on the Continent enabled him to make such comparisons, support Tony

Bareham's statement that Lever had become 'more European than his readership could well stomach'.[38] They also resulted in the consistently mixed reaction to his writings. While the essays are peppered with remarks unpalatable to many English readers, however, their overall tone is very far from being universally confrontational. Despite his avowal that his critics should have his 'pickles' 'hotter than ever',[39] it sometimes seems that Lever wished to be conciliatory. In 'An Immoral Consideration', for example, he defends the press, maintaining, in the face of his persistent condemnation of it, that it is both amusing and instructive. In this recognition we can identify the exile's honest acknowledgment of his reliance upon the newspapers as a source of both information and subject matter for his essays.

In his letters to Blackwood, Lever exhibited both his enthusiasm for essay-writing and his confidence in his abilities, even going so far as to claim that, 'I am sure such sketches are far more my "speciality" than story-writing'.[40] We may feel that this is over-stating the case, but his mature essays have considerable merit; certainly, they reveal no hint of the 'brain bankruptcy' which he so much feared in his declining years.[41] In their observation of men and manners, in political analysis, and most particularly in their skilful use of personal anecdote and experience, they remain both entertaining and a useful mechanism by which to gauge the workings of Lever's mind and the huge extent of his development. The critic of his work would be wrong to grant them a position of too much prominence, but equally mistaken in ignoring them altogether. While *Nuts and Nutcrackers* might be dismissed as immature, ephemeral and sometimes offensive, the best of *Cornelius O'Dowd* exhibits a maturity and humanity reminiscent of his finest novels.

6

LEVER'S ANTI-HEROINES

– I –

We have already witnessed Lever's ability to achieve centrality for his female characters, sometimes in their own right, and sometimes in terms of their influence on the individual motivations of other characters. As time progressed he showed an ever-increasing willingness to push his male characters to the very periphery of the action and to assign the central role within his novels to the women. Tony Bareham has offered us an analysis of this process:

> as Lever's primary attention turned away from the young men and towards the womenfolk in his novels, we can see another move away from an obvious centre. He ceases to relish describing the masculine world of affairs and decision-making associated with the military mess or camp, and moves towards a series of stories where, without the control, wisdom and maturity of the females, the world would collapse.[1]

Even in the earlier novels we can discover an increasing concern with the female characters. In *The O'Donoghue*, for instance, Kate O'Donoghue, Mark's primary source of motivation, is not the mere shadowy outline of idealised feminine virtue to be found in the first novels, but a passionate being of flesh and blood with her own highly-developed system of beliefs. Mary Martin, in *The Martins of Cro' Martin*, is the first example of a fully centralised heroine, whose actions form the very hub of the narrative and from this point onward to his final novel, *Lord Kilgobbin*, the female characters are absolutely integral to the progression of nearly all Lever's major fictions.

It would be a mistake, however, to assume that all of his heroines are forces for good, or, indeed, that in their own right they can be considered 'good' in any sense of the word. In *Lord Kilgobbin* as well as in a further two consecutive novels of his late maturity, *Sir Brook Fossbrooke* and *The Bramleighs of Bishop's Folly*, we are presented with complex studies of women who in their motivations and actions might best be described as anti-heroines. Through his examination of the lives and marriages of essentially unsympathetic women Lever offers us some of his most pungent criticisms of a society which he considered deeply restrictive in the roles which it assigned to its womenfolk.

– II –

In February 1865, writing to his publisher, John Blackwood, of his new novel, *Sir Brook Fossbrooke*, Lever expressed his desire 'to write you the best story in my market,' adding with his customary diffidence, 'that is, if I have a market'.[2] In fact, despite the usual difficulties in its composition, bouts of ill-health and a frequently expressed need for Blackwood's approbation, by the time of the novel's completion he felt that he had created one of his best fictions. Certainly he had made considerable efforts in its composition, and had devoted much energy to both plot and characterisation, calling it 'the most carefully written of my works'.[3] Despite these expressions of satisfaction, however, Fitzpatrick tells us that 'with readers it never had much popularity'[4] and contemporary reviews were so unenthusiastic that Lever 'reiterated his suspicion that there was personal ill-will toward him in the London press'.[5]

Although A. Norman Jeffares has defended the novel, claiming that it 'provides us with a searching analysis of the Anglo-Irish decline as well as of English misrule',[6] in fact, upon reading *Sir Brook Fossbrooke*, the modern reader is likely to discover one of the few occasions upon which he will agree with the predominantly negative criticisms. With its apparent lack of direction, and Lever's infuriating habit of introducing characters only to let them disappear for lengthy stretches of the narrative, the novel is, structurally, one of the weakest to issue from his pen. Early in its composition he voiced his wish 'to do the thing well,' but admitted that 'I have not yet got the stick by the handle'.[7] Whereas, in many of his works, an early uncertainty developed into a strong exposition of character and a confident narrative progression, in *Sir Brook Fossbrooke* we might well feel that he never did manage to grasp 'the stick by the handle' and that, in his affection for this novel, he was correct when he stated:

it's no new error of mine to find good in things of my writing that nobody but myself has ever discovered.[8]

Bearing in mind such later novels as *The Bramleighs of Bishop's Folly* and *Lord Kilgobbin*, his belief that 'I don't think I shall do better than *Sir Brook*'[9] seems unjustifiably pessimistic.

In his penetrating article on 'Charles Lever and the Outsider',[10] Tony Bareham has drawn attention to Lever's use of the device of the 'false ending'; in *Sir Brook Fossbrooke* we find instead the 'false beginning' as characters are introduced whose real influence on the direction of the plot is minimal. It is not until chapter eighteen and the introduction of Colonel Sewell and his wife Lucy that the action is truly under way, and despite Lever's satisfaction with his depiction of Baron Lendrick, 'a portrait on which I expended a great deal of time and paint',[11] it is in his analysis of the characters of this couple and of their unhappy marriage that the reader's interest finds its centre and the novel as a whole its most successful components.

In Lucy Sewell Lever attempted the portrayal of an entirely new kind of heroine. She is a beautiful, intelligent and graceful woman, but one who has been corrupted, or, rather, one whose innate depravity of character has been nurtured by her nefarious husband. In his first description of her the eponymous, though often absent, hero of the novel outlines Lucy Sewell's early career, her decline from naive and artless schoolgirl to calculating and artful woman of the world:

'What! it is incredible – surely that is not she who once was Lucy Dillon – that bold-faced woman with lustrous eyes and rouged cheeks – brilliant, indeed, and beautiful, but not the beauty that is allied to the thought of virtue – whose every look is a wile, whose every action is entanglement.'[12]

To emphasise the depravity of her nature, Mrs Sewell is contrasted throughout the novel with her rather colourless namesake Lucy Lendrick, her wantonness placed opposite to the *ingenue's* simplicity. But though, with his knowledge of her past, Sir Brook is able to paint his old acquaintance in the most unflattering light, the reaction of the other protagonists depends largely upon their age and experience.

Dr Lendrick, the son whom the Baron has disowned, despite his seclusion from the world, detects almost immediately that her apparent simplicity 'only covers a deep knowledge of life and the world'.[13] Furthermore, despite her obvious fear of her husband he discovers them exchanging 'the very look that two accomplices might have interchanged in a moment when they could not communicate more freely'.[14] Above all, the doctor is anxious that his daughter and Mrs Sewell should be kept apart, fearing the effects of the latter's worldliness on his daughter's innocence. We find, of course, that his fears are unfounded, and that the younger Lucy's virtue and truly Victorian primness are beyond any threat posed by the roué. Lucy Lendrick is not, however, the only innocent who falls under Mrs Sewell's shadow. Lucy's lover, Lionel Trafford, proves rather more susceptible to her beguiling combination of listlessness and coquetry and it is in Mrs Sewell's ensnaring the young soldier and, more particularly, in her ill-dissembled triumph over the younger woman that her worst characteristics are revealed to the reader:

> 'If I were treacherous, I would not make this avowal to you. I should be satisfied with the advantage I possessed, and employ it to my benefit. Perhaps with any other woman than yourself I should play this part, – with you I neither can nor will. I will declare to you frankly and at once, you have lost the game and I have won it.'[15]

Lucy, whose wariness of Mrs Sewell has been growing apace, is disgusted by the mock-friendliness, the barely concealed exultation expressed in her name-sake's communication, and the reader shares her revulsion.

The greatest strength of the characterisation, though, lies in the fact that the reader's reaction to the anti-heroine is not simple abhorrence. There is something both appealing and sympathetic in her make-up. In his correspondence with John Blackwood, Lever described his intentions with regard to the ambivalence of our reaction to her nature:

> The character of Mrs Sewell was a great difficulty – that is, the attempt to show how mere gracefulness could appear something better, and that a woman might be as depraved as a man without forfeiting to a great extent our sympathy, and even something stronger.[16]

Lucy Sewell, though guilty of connivance in her husband's strategies, is also a victim. She is an intelligent and gifted woman caught in a marriage in which the predominant emotion is mutual hatred. Each partner despises and loathes the other and yet there is also a mutual dependence; as Sewell expresses it, 'there are no two people in Europe ought to understand each other better than we do'.[17] Throughout the novel the brutality of Sewell's language and actions are unmitigated, but it is clear that despite years of the same treatment his wife is not immune to the wounds which he maliciously inflicts:

> She grasped the table convulsively to steady herself, and in so doing threw it down, and the whole tea equipage with it.
>
> 'Yes,' continued he, as though responding to this evidence of emotion on her part – 'yes: it pushed one's patience pretty hard to be obliged to sit under such criticism.'
>
> 'And what obliged you, sir? was it fear?'
>
> 'Yes, madam, you have guessed it. I was afraid – terribly afraid to own I was your husband.'[18]

Sewell relies upon his wife's attractiveness to ensnare the unsuspecting, but her success in obeying his commands results not in his approbation but rather in further slights and abuse, the product of his own sexual jealousy. The Colonel's treatment of his wife, and no doubt the inherent features of her own character, have made her deeply cynical. Her condemnation of the married state and of the woman's role within it is uncompromising: 'The thing that we call love, in married life has an existence only a little beyond that of the bouquet you carried to the wedding-breakfast; and it would be unreasonable in a woman to expect it'.[19]

Sir Brook's reaction to Lucy Sewell is agonised revulsion. He remembers what she was once, sees what she has become and recoils. Her attitude towards her guardian and god-parent is equally absolute: she evinces nothing but a passionate hatred for him. Ironically, it is in this hatred that we see that she is not entirely shameless. Sir Brook represents conscience and causes her to recollect the past and her benign and loving father. Wherever possible she attempts to blacken Sir Brook's name, both to discredit any criticisms which he might make of her, but surely also to convince herself that this arbiter of morality is not so far distanced from her own fallen condition. There is a significant difference between the Colonel and his wife: while he calculates with the coolness of a professional, she still allows her passions to affect her actions. When a plot of his devising fails, Sewell reacts with a certain blasphemous stoicism and concentrates upon the formulation of his next scheme. For instance, in his attempt to extort money from Trafford for his supposed dalliance with his wife, Sewell looks upon the incident as a business transaction. However, when it becomes clear that Trafford has seen his weakness in becoming so involved and that his loyalties truly lie with Lucy Lendrick, the older woman gives herself over completely to outraged vanity:

'Am I to tell you what this man said to me? Is that what you mean?' said she, in a voice that almost hissed with passion.

'Better not, perhaps,' replied he, calmly, 'if the very recollection overcame you so completely.'

'That is to say, it is better I should bear the insult how I may than reveal it to one who will not resent it.'

'When you say resent, do you intend I should call him out? – fight him?'

'If I were the husband instead of the wife, it is what I should do – ay,' cried she, wildly, 'and thank Fortune that gave me the chance.'

'I don't think I'm going to show any such gratitude,' said he, with a cold grin.[20]

Passionate and proud, Lucy Sewell cannot respond with the cold and calculating professional villainy of her husband, her nature does not lend itself to the role which has been created for her by marriage.

There are other moments in which Mrs Sewell's character is seen to be ill-suited to the part allotted to her. In her clearly genuine love for her children, for instance, we witness a relationship in which her otherwise strangled affections are permitted an outlet; and in his casually expressed favouritism towards one of his two daughters Sewell unintentionally augments his wife's loathing:

> His wife's eyes followed him as he went, and never did a human face exhibit a stronger show of repressed passion than hers, as, with closely-compressed lips and staring eyes, she watched him as he passed out.[21]

Again, in her refusal to aid her husband in his attempts to fraudulently ascertain the contents of the critically ill Baron Lendrick's will, the villainess reveals a moral rectitude and determination seldom apparent in her relations with the other characters within the novel.[22]

The final, and perhaps most potent, analysis of Mrs Sewell's emotions comes as she awaits the outcome of the duel with Lionel Trafford, in which she has blackmailed her husband to become a principal. Her insistence on the duel is due entirely to her injured pride, to the fact that Trafford has preferred Lucy Lendrick to herself, even though in originally making advances toward Trafford she was merely obeying the injunctions of her husband. The publicity which an exchange of shots will produce can only be damaging to her reputation but her passion has become so intense that caution is thrown to the winds, everything is of secondary importance compared with her vengeance on the young lovers:

> 'How absurd!' broke she out, 'are they who imagine that one only wants to be avenged on those who hate us! It is the wrongs done by people who are indifferent to us, and who, in search of their own objects, bestow no thought upon us – these are the ills that cannot be forgiven. I never hated a human being – and there have been some who have earned my hate – as I hate this girl; and just as I feel the injustice of the sentiment, so does it eat deeper and deeper into my heart.'[23]

Lucy's lack of interest bites deepest; the fact that a simple country girl, untutored in the ways of the world, has the daring to be actually indifferent. There is a powerful and undeniable reality in this analysis of motivation: in the fact that Mrs Sewell recognises the injustice of her hatred and through the recognition magnifies her antipathy. The end to her impatience is a telegram from the Colonel announcing that he has 'thought better of it' and that, therefore, the duel has not taken place. After her impatience, this news results in a stunned torpor:

She sat pondering over these words till the paper became blurred and blotted by her tears as they rolled heavily along her cheeks, and dropped with a distinct sound. She was not conscious that she wept. It was not grief that moved her; it was the blankness of despair – the sense of hopelessness that comes over the heart when life no longer offers a plan or a project, but presents a wearyful road to be travelled, uncheered and dreary. [24]

Unable to achieve her ends by direct action, constrained by the conventions of Victorian society, Lucy Sewell is left to bemoan her powerlessness and, like so many of Lever's heroines, to wish that, without losing her own native courage and determination, she was a man with a man's freedom of action. Finally, her plans for revenge in ruins and the young lovers reunited, she resigns herself to following her husband to Boulogne, a move dictated by the propinquity of their corrupt natures.

The characters of Colonel and Mrs Sewell and the portrayal of their marriage of convenience are the redeeming merits of *Sir Brook Fossbrooke*. Without them the novel would hardly be worthy of attention. Though indisputably the villainess of the piece, Lucy Sewell is in no way stereotypical. Lever does not condone her actions, which are almost exclusively designed for the betterment of her and her husband's condition, but there is nonetheless a sympathy and understanding in his analysis of her character. The marriage itself, with its mutual hatred, verbal and physical violence, but also its moments of collusion and mutual understanding make it a fascinating study. Once Lever had introduced the couple his attention seldom strayed from them, they become in reality the axis upon which the plot turns and the mining adventures of Sir Brook are little more than irritating distractions. Had he introduced the couple earlier and from the outset built his novel around them, there can be little doubt that he would have succeeded in writing the 'best story' in his market.

– III –

Lever's next published novel, *The Bramleighs of Bishop's Folly*, is in all respects superior to *Sir Brook Fossbrooke* and might justly be considered one of the finest works of his late maturity. Lever himself was not enthusiastic and found the process of composition tedious, admitting 'a daily increasing repugnance to writing'.[25] Despite his pessimism, however, the novel represents a further development in his style and Fitzpatrick's assessment, though brief, remains largely accurate:

Lever now, almost for the first time, succeeded in producing an elaborate plot, the mystery of which was so astutely veiled that, although simple and natural enough, the reader finds himself at last quite taken by surprise.[26]

The novel's carefully constructed plot represents a significant departure from its author's normally haphazard methods of composition, though, to the modern reader, what Fitzpatrick describes as 'simple and natural enough' might seem to be another example of Victorian melodrama.

Like so many of Lever's works, *The Bramleighs of Bishop's Folly* benefits from a number of beautifully drawn characters, from the careful analysis of their individual motivations and from the web of relationships subsisting between them. As with *Sir Brook Fossbrooke*, the relationship which demands the most attention is a marriage – that of Marion Bramleigh and her diplomat husband, Lord Culduff. In the female partner of the union we discover another complex portrait of Victorian womanhood in one of its less common guises. Lucy Sewell was a cynical adventuress, more or less inured to the villainies of her husband; Marion Bramleigh shares the earlier character's cynicism and intelligence, but rather than employ them in financially motivated criminal intrigues, she utilises her attributes to secure a goal shared by innumerable other nineteenth century women: a match which is both materially and socially advantageous.

The Bramleighs are essentially nouveau riche. Owing their very considerable wealth first to brewing and more latterly to banking, they are an example of the growing class of Victorian entrepreneurs who seek respectability and social acceptance through disassociating themselves from the foundations of their opulence. Various attempts to achieve this goal have been made: the head of the family has purchased a militia colonelcy, has married the scion of a noble house, purchased a country estate and contested an election; but each strategy has failed. The Colonel and his second wife live separately, in the election he attained a reputation for radicalism through supporting the Whigs in a profoundly Tory county and the need to save face after political failure necessitated the sale of the Herefordshire estate. The move to Ireland and the purchase of Castello, or 'Bishop's Folly', is a last ditch effort to attain social ascendancy.

Marion Bramleigh is the eldest daughter of the house; beautiful, proud and imperious, her philosophy of life is early expounded:

This was Marion's code: it took three generations to make a family; the first must be wealthy; the second, by the united force of money and ability, secure a certain station of power and social influence; the third must fortify these by marriages – marriages of distinction; after which mere time would do the rest.[27]

This philosophy permits neither sentiment nor love: the younger Bramleighs have a duty to dignify their family, and this obligation outweighs any personal preferences as to marriage. That Jack, the youngest son, should wish to marry Julia L'Estrange, the penniless parson's sister, is to Marion perfectly horrifying. Enjoying all the trappings of wealth, the family's socially ambivalent position remains a source of extreme discomfort and one which must be surmounted at whatever cost.

The introduction to the family circle of the diplomatist Lord Culduff provides Marion with the opportunity for her own sacrifice to the dictates of her philosophy. She is in her early twenties, while Culduff is approaching seventy, though tortuous devotions to his toilette can, in a complimentary light, enable him to pass for forty. A vain, shallow, preening and self-deluding fop there seems little in Culduff which might appeal to a woman of spirit and intelligence, and yet:

He was a great favourite with women. Old ladies regarded him as a model of good *ton*; younger ones discovered other qualities in him that amused them as much. His life had been anything but blameless, but he had contrived to make the world believe he was more sinned against than sinning. . . .

He was, in a word, the incarnation of a very well-bred selfishness, that had learned how much it redounds to a man's personal comfort that he is popular, and that even a weak swimmer who goes with the tide, makes a better figure than the strongest and bravest who attempts to stem the current.[28]

The fourteenth holder of the viscountancy, a distinguished member of the diplomatic corps with access to the salons of high society, Lord Culduff represents all that is desirable to the ambitious Marion, though in years he is old enough to be her grandfather.

Unlike *Sir Brook Fossbrooke*, in which Colonel and Lucy Sewell are introduced to the reader as a married couple, in *The Bramleighs of Bishop's Folly* we witness the progression of the courtship between Marion and Culduff. While she is attracted by the social benefits which such an alliance would confer, he is tempted by her personal fortune of twenty-thousand pounds, as well as being unable to abandon his accustomed habits of flirtation. Further, when his overly subtle advances are misinterpreted and therefore ignored, his pride is piqued:

What Marion's manner towards him might be in future, was also a painful reflection. It would naturally be a triumphant incident in her life to have rejected such an offer. Would she be eager to parade this fact before the world? Would she try to let people know that she had refused him? This was possible. He felt that such a slight would tarnish the glory of his life, whose boast it was to have done many things that were actually wicked, but not one that was merely weak.[29]

There is certainly no passion and, indeed, very little interest for Culduff in this courtship; he conducts it because it is his custom. To be fair to Marion, there is evidence of a greater emotional involvement on her part, though it is expressed merely as a result of jealousy when Culduff pays a compliment to Julia L'Estrange's beauty.[30] All in all, the courtship is one of calculation: Marion will achieve the unquestioned respectability which she craves while Culduff's interest is essentially a pecuniary one, more than a little tinged by vanity.

When the offer of marriage is finally made and accepted in an atmosphere tainted by the mortal illness of Colonel Bramleigh, the reaction of Augustus, Marion's eldest brother, is one of disgusted astonishment. Her response to his outcry is an uncompromising avowal of her motivation:

'I am not one of your love-in-a-cottage young ladies, Gusty. I am, I must own it, excessively worldly. Whatever happiness I could propose to myself in life is essentially united to a certain ambition. We have as many of the advantages of mere wealth as most people . . . and what do they do for us? They permit us simply to enter the lists with a set of people who have high-stepping horses and powdered lacqueys like ourselves, but who are no more the world, no more society, than one of papa's Indiamen is a ship of the Royal Navy.'[31]

For Marion, such a marriage represents all that is most desirable in life and, in expressing her satisfaction, she once again gives voice to the truly Leverian awareness of the bitter sexual inequality inherent in nineteenth century society:

'these things are hard to bear for a man, for a woman they are intolerable. She has not the hundred and one careers in life in which individual distinction can obliterate the claims of station. She has but one stage – the salon; but, to her, this narrow world, soft-carpeted and damask-curtained, is a very universe, and without the recognised stamp of a certain rank in it, she is absolutely nothing.'[32]

The sentiments shared by so many of Lever's female characters, both sympathetic and unsympathetic, are paraded once again and though Marion does not actually state in unequivocal terms her desire to be a man, this wish for her is expressed by her father who recognises her superior abilities and her fitness to undertake the business of the bank.[33]

Despite her confidence in her talents and in her fitness for a higher position in society, there are indications that Marion's conviction is less securely founded than she herself believes. Early in the novel, before Lord Culduff's first arrival at Bishop's Folly, there is a discussion as to his accommodation in the house. Naturally, the best and most lavish guest-rooms are allotted to the noble visitor:

The keys of this precious suite were in Marion's keeping, and as she walked through the rooms with Temple, and expiated on the reckless expenditure bestowed upon them, she owned that for any less distinguished guest than the great diplomatist she would never have consented to their being opened.[34]

The value of the rooms' fittings is undeniable, but in her over-awareness of their worth there is something approximating ill-breeding, a lack of comfortable familiarity. It is in faults such as these, and in Culduff's remarking upon them, that the seeds of acrimonious marital discord are soon to be found:

> 'My very great admiration had not blinded me as to certain peculiarities, let me call them, of manner; and if my vanity induced me to believe that I should be able to correct them, it is only my error.'
>
> 'I protest, my lord, if my temper sustain me under such insult as this, I think I might be acquitted of ill-breeding.'
>
> 'I live in the hope, madam, that such a charge would be impossible.'
>
> 'I suppose you mean,' said she, with a sneering smile, 'when I have taken more lessons, – when I have completed the course of instruction you so courteously began with me yesterday?'
>
> 'Precisely, madam, precisely.'[35]

Throughout such scenes Marion exhibits great spirit and strength of will, obviously despising the husband who can so callously belittle her, and yet she is also careful to profit from his instruction, however unfeelingly bestowed. No sympathy exists between them and their private life remains a hollow shell, but Marion succeeds in attaining the position which she sought and Culduff is happy to bask in the glory reflected by his young wife's beauty and presence. The only substantial link between the two is their passionate care for outward appearances and for the unstinting respect of their peers; each will support the other because their own individual standing depends upon it. Even so, Marion is made to feel her position as an outsider when Culduff and her high-born stepmother enjoy a *tête-à-tête*.[36]

Despite their incompatibilities in age and temperament, we are given to understand that the marriage will be, in worldly terms, a success and Lever admonishes us to accept the sincerity of Marion's last statement within the novel:

> She was – and it was a pet phrase with her – 'resigned' to everything: resigned to Lord Culduff's being made a grand cross and an ambassador, with the reasonable prospect of an earldom; resigned to her own great part – and was it not a great part? – in this advancement; resigned to be an ambassadress! That she was resigned to the ruin and downfall of her family, especially if they should have the delicacy and good taste to hide themselves somewhere, and not obtrude that ruin and downfall on the world, was plainly manifest.[37]

Marion's goal in life has never been under question, and through marriage to Lord Culduff that goal has, in essence, been achieved. Love has nothing to do with their relationship; it is true that she expected common courtesy from her husband, but his failure in this respect and the trials which she is made to endure in private are rendered acceptable by her social success. There is no cause for regret and no regret is expressed. In his essay on 'Charles Lever and the Outsider', Tony Bareham has offered us a summary of Marion's position by the end of the novel:

> By marriage she has become part of the diplomatic world where she appears to be absolutely at the centre of things. In reality, however, she is completely frozen out not only from her wretched husband's affections, but from any real central position in the fashionable world she hankered for and equally, from the increasing domestic warmth of her own brothers and sisters.[38]

At first sight, this analysis seems perfectly accurate, but in our appalled reaction to it we presuppose a common human warmth in Marion's make-up. In fact, a thorough reading of the novel denies such a constituent in her character. Marion is driven purely by the fire of social ambition, an ambition for ostensible acceptance into the realm of high society – though there is evidence that she has never doubted her natural equality with such society:

> She was no convert to his opinions as to the necessity of any peculiar stratagem in the campaign of life. She had seen the house in town crowded with very great and distinguished company; she had observed how wealth asserted itself in society, and she could not perceive that in their acceptance by the world, there was any, the slightest deficiency of deference and respect. If they had failed in their county experiment in England, it was, she thought, because her father rashly took up an extreme position in politics.[39]

If Marion is at all affected by her self-imposed exclusion from her family circle, there is certainly no explicit recognition of the fact, nor indeed is such a recognition even implied. Hearts and souls are of very little consequence to her, unquestioned social equality is everything.

Marion Bramleigh is, in essence, a deeply unsympathetic character, cold-hearted and ruthlessly ambitious. Even when she suffers under the deliberately inflicted slights of her husband the reader is more likely to feel that she is reaping what she has sown, than to pity her. However, there are very real strengths in her character and ones which deserve our attention. There is, for instance, no denying her belief in her philosophy – a philosophy which she has boldly proclaimed despite the objections of her siblings. She refuses to be led, to be submissive or to play the hypocrite. Furthermore, she firmly believes that what she does, she does to benefit the whole family, though her subsequent willingness to leave the remaining Bramleighs to ruin and possible destitution effectively negates any credit attaching to such a conviction. Her independence and ability to bear censure unflinchingly are also characteristics in her favour, as is the intelligence recognised by her father. Her desire for social ascendancy is dictated largely by her position as a woman trapped by the mores of a deeply restrictive society. Had Marion been able to follow a career in banking, a career for which her father has already identified her eminent suitability, her comparatively hollow social ambition would probably never have surfaced.

– IV –

In describing the moral dynamics behind the characterisation of *Lord Kilgobbin*, Lever stated:

> I verily believe that in my sketch of ordinary life, the transcendently good will occupy a small space, and the stage be filled by the people of mixed motives, not very wicked or the reverse, but doing a variety of inconvenient, and some positively bad things; out of temper, passing resentment, imaginary injury, wounded self-love, and worse than all – hang them – pure idleness! It is of these the kingdom of the world is made up, and we know it is not heaven![40]

The novel contains one 'transcendently good' heroine, Mathew Kearney's daughter, Kate; Nina Kostalergi's motives, meanwhile, are sufficiently 'mixed' to earn her a place among Lever's anti-heroines. Although they stand at different extremes of the moral spectrum, it is absolutely typical of Lever's portrayal of women that Nina and Kate both evince more energy and determination than all, bar one, of the many male characters in *Lord Kilgobbin*.

Nina is, perhaps, the most morally ambivalent of all Lever's female characters: and, at the same time, the most convincing. Her every action is, in some measure, the product of caprice, there is no goal to her existence and no overwhelming passion. She is, in all senses, an outsider: the daughter of the impecunious and worldly 'Prince of Delos' she inhabits the borderland of respectable poverty in which the prime motivation of existence is the maintenance of appearances:

> Nina emerges from this rather shopsoiled background a tainted character. Despite her charisma and courage, there is always something about her which seems not quite straight and limpid. Her arrival as a refugee/guest at Kilgobbin castle allows Lever splendid scope to develop these contrasts between Nina and the transparent Kate Kearney. This is a genuinely creative development of the Becky/Amelia relationship in *Vanity Fair*.[41]

In Continental society she is marginalised by her poverty, while in Ireland her foreign manners set her apart:

> 'She is not one of us, Kate: none of her ways or thoughts are ours, nor would they suit us.'[42]

She can never be entirely integrated into either society, not least because she is herself unwilling to make the necessary concessions to conformity.

Kate Kearney is cast in the mould of the self-sacrificing Mary Martin: there is a very real centre to her existence and that centre is the struggle for the effective and responsible management of her father's shattered estate. In the wake of decades of neglect and the wilfully obscure mismanagement of Peter Gill, Kearney's steward, this struggle is both bewildering and exhausting:

> Kate, still dressed, had thrown herself on her bed, and was sound asleep. The table was covered with account-books and papers: tax receipts, law notices, and tenants' letters lay littered about, showing what had been the task she was last engaged on; and her heavy breathing told the exhaustion which it had left behind it.[43]

Nina, on the other hand, has no real hub to her existence; instead she revolves around a series of flirtations with whichever men enter her sphere: Dick Kearney, Cecil Walpole, Joe Atlee, Daniel Donogan, Gorman O'Shea and Captain Curtis. She acts upon the whim of the moment and, in her wilfulness, will brook no restraint. When Kate asks her to spare the feelings of her brother, for instance, her response is:

> 'And so I shall, Kate, if you don't dictate or order me. Leave me quite to myself and I shall be most merciful.'[44]

For the most part she deliberately fascinates them for no better reason than because she can, although she admits the possibility, indeed the 'ecstasy', of a reciprocal affection or love:

> 'Can you men never be brought to see that we are not all alike to each of you; that our natures have their separate watch-words, and that the soul which would vibrate with tenderness to this, is to that, a dead and senseless thing, with no trace nor touch of feeling about it?'
> 'I only believe this in part.'
> 'Believe it wholly, then, or own that you know nothing of love – no more than do those countless thousands who go through life and never taste its real ecstasy, nor its real sorrow.'[45]

Despite the acknowledgment of such a possibility, however, her flirtations are usually empty things devoid of passion and interest. It is a code of behaviour which appalls Kate and which pushes the two girls apart, despite their genuine affection for one another. It is not too much to suggest that, although Nina has none of the confirmed vices of Lucy Sewell, her flirtations being as much the product of boredom as of whim, she does reveal the germ of Mrs Sewell's corruption, a germ which, in the right soil, might prove only too capable of growth. As the earlier anti-heroine reveals her moral decay nowhere more strongly than in her vengefulness toward Lucy Lendrick and her lover, Trafford, Nina reacts similarly to the unintentional slight of Gorman O'Shea. Recovering from the delirium induced by a near-fatal assault, in the darkness of his sick-room, Gorman mistakes Nina for Kate and warns her against her cousin. Nina makes no attempt to tell the invalid of her identity before his unintentional indiscretion and, despite having received his confidence under false pretences, bears a grudge:

> It was with passionate eagerness Nina set off in search of Kate. Why she should have felt herself wronged, outraged, insulted even, is not so easy to say, nor shall I attempt any analysis of the complex web of sentiments which, so to say, spread itself over her faculties. The man who had so wounded her self-love had been at her feet, he had followed her in her walks, hung over the piano as she sang – shown by a thousand signs that sort of devotion by which men intimate that their lives have but one solace, one ecstasy, one joy. By what treachery had he been moved to all this, if he really loved another? That he was simply amusing himself with the sort of flirtation she herself could take up as a mere pastime was not to be believed. That the worshipper should be insincere in his worship was too dreadful to be thought of.[46]

Nina's anger at being considered a 'pastime' is hypocritical in the extreme since she has herself played, in exactly the same manner, with Gorman's and many another's affections, but it is no less realistic for all that. No less realistic than Lucy Sewell's savage, indeed murderous, rage at Trafford's rejection of her, though her beguilement of his affections had been dictated purely by her husband's criminal intrigues. Nina is perhaps not so knowledgeable of herself as Lucy, her passion is not further inflamed by an awareness of its injustice, but it is as genuine:

> 'How shall I punish him for this? How shall I make him remember whom it is he has insulted?' repeated she over and over to herself as she went.[47]

Her words bear a marked similarity to those of the dyed-in-the-wool villainess, Madame Cleremont in the immediately preceding novel, *That Boy of Norcott's*.[48] Unlike Madame Cleremont, however, Nina is no two-dimensional personification of evil, though she visits her anger on the affectionate and generous Kate. Her character is an altogether more complex and convincing study of caprice and irrational, spontaneous prejudice and by developing it in this manner, Lever serves no contrived or melodramatic device of plot. There are no significant ramifications to Nina's injustice but the incident serves to emphasise the capricious nature of her character.

She is, in some ways, a deliberate development of the tourist in Ireland convention, as used in the fictions of Maria Edgeworth, Lady Morgan and Charles Maturin. In the same spirit of enquiry exhibited by her predecessors, and with all their ingenuousness, she at one point states:

> 'But I do want to go to the bottom of this question. I will insist on learning why people rebel here.'[49]

Unlike most earlier examples, however, Nina has no strong preconceptions of the island and its inhabitants, whether good or bad. Her passionate espousal of the cause of liberty has been noticed in an earlier chapter, as have her similarities with her prototype, Kate O'Donoghue. It is this espousal which brings her closer to the Fenian, Daniel Donogan:

> 'Do you know Mademoiselle, that this same Donogan was a man of fortune, and in all the society of the first men at Oxford when – a mere boy at the time – he became a rebel?'
> 'How nice of him, what a fine fellow!'
> 'I'd say what a fool,' continued Curtis. 'He had no need to risk his neck to achieve a station, the thing was done for him. He had a good house and a good estate in Kilkenny; I have caught salmon in the river that washes the foot of his lawn.'
> 'And what has become of it; does he still own it?'
> 'Not an acre – not a rood of it; sold off every square yard of it to throw the money into the Fenian treasury. Rifled artillery, Colt's revolvers, Remington's and Parrot guns have walked off with the broad acres.'
> 'Fine fellow – a fine fellow!' cried Nina, enthusiastically.[50]

Her movement toward the role of anti-heroine is revealed most clearly through her fascination with the cause and in her subsequent betrayal of these feelings. Having exhibited an unlooked for sincerity, Nina also reveals a willingness to compromise it by becoming engaged to Cecil Walpole, the viceroy's private secretary, and a prime mover in the government's machinations:

> 'The man is a greater fool than I thought him, and mistakes his native weakness of mind for originality. If you had heard the imbecile nonsense he talked to me for political shrewdness, and when he had shown me what a very poor creature he was, he made me the offer of himself! This was so far honest and aboveboard. It was saying, in so many words, "You see, I am a bankrupt".'[51]

By utilising her relationship with Walpole to assist Donogan to escape the pursuit of the police, Nina shows that she retains a commitment to her beliefs and an interest in the Fenian's fate, but at the same time she is willing to compromise herself by marriage to a man who personifies the antithesis to these beliefs and whom she despises. To Nina, marriage to Walpole presents the conventional escape from undistinguished and uncertain spinsterhood. From a social aspect, the match is also extremely desirable:

'is it anything else than one of those mercenary attachments that you young ladies understand better, far better, than the most worldly-minded father or mother of us all?'[52]

The answer to Mathew Kearney's question, must be a negative. Nina has no particular fear of poverty, but her essential ostracism from society in Italy has produced an understandable desire for security; like Marion Bramleigh, she sees marriage as a means to an end: that end being stability and an unimpeachable social rank. She is the female counterpart of the Nationalist, Joe Atlee. Furthermore, as he compromises his principles by becoming a servant to an administration which he abhors, she becomes engaged to a man whom she cannot respect and who holds views which are the very antithesis of her own. Atlee's betrayal of his beliefs is total and by the end of the novel he has become a self-deluding coxcomb who has alienated our sympathies irredeemably. Nina, on the other hand, teeters on the brink of an equally catastrophic decision but at the last moment retreats and is saved by marriage to Donogan. Although she never quite passes the point of no return, her salvation is not the result of any significant development on her part – rather, it is as much the product of caprice as even her most shallow and transient flirtation. That she is attracted to Donogan, there can be no doubt. That she finds him in all ways superior to the effete and listless young men who drift in and out of the circle of Kilgobbin Castle is equally sure: but one of her primary motivations in accepting the match is the power of her own vanity, a fact which Donogan himself recognises and uses. He knows that he must make elopement with him more appealing to her self-love than the more conventional match with Walpole:

To share the destiny of such a man was to ensure a life that could not pass unrecorded. There might be storm, and even shipwreck, but there was notoriety – perhaps even fame! . . .
   The whirlwind rapidity of his eloquence also moved her, and the varied arguments he addressed, now to her heroism, now to her self-sacrifice, now to the power of her beauty, now to the contempt she felt for the inglorious lives of common-place people – the ignoble herd, who passed unnoticed.[53]

In essence, Nina rejects one contract for another more exciting, though more risky. Mutual love as a constituent in the match remains doubtful and more hangs in the balance than material success. One of her prime motivations is ambition, the quest for recognition which in traditional Victorian terms would be considered a male preserve and which Nina, despite her abilities can only approach through allegiance to a man. In departing for America with Donogan, she casts aside many of the conventions of respectability but she fails to make that last break and instead seeks 'notoriety – perhaps even fame' by linking herself with the one man in her acquaintance who promises the exceptional. The match does not therefore align with the Victorian expectation of 'love and marriage licences' but in a calculated risk which bears little relation to the romantic expectations of Lever's audience. As the shadow of continuing unrest and possible Nationalist retribution against Gorman O'Shea hangs over Kate's nuptials, there is a cloud above Nina's future and each heroine faces an uncertainty which reveals the mature Lever's unwillingness, or inability, to pander to the nineteenth century convention of the happy ending.

– V –

In his creation of Lucy Sewell and Marion Bramleigh, Lever exhibited his ability to engage the interest of his readers in largely unsympathetic portrayals of womanhood. Furthermore, he revealed through their histories how the conditions of Victorian society can repress and reshape character. Both women are eminently intelligent and attractive, one is fundamentally cold in temperament, the other is passionate, but both are prevented from finding a legitimate and worthwhile conduit for their abilities. Ironically, it is Lucy Sewell, the woman whose motivation is overtly criminal, who succeeds in attaining the greatest degree of our sympathy through her passion and through the day-to-day brutality of her domestic circumstances. Marion's nature is too cold, too calculating to allow any real empathy, though we can appreciate her qualities and the fact that her abilities, in another society, might be far more profitably directed. In Lucy we discover vacillation, her criminality is tempered by humanity and conscience and by her genuine love for her children; Marion, however, in her unswerving purpose sometimes resembles an automaton.

Both *Sir Brook Fossbrooke* and *The Bramleighs of Bishop's Folly* contain fascinating studies of barren marriages, in which mutual affection and regard between the partners are wholly absent. In each the wife is subjected to abuse, whether mental or physical, and yet in both there exists a remarkable element of connivance: Marion has married Culduff for rank and without supporting his position her own is forfeit, while the fates of Sewell and Lucy, it seems, are so inextricably intertwined in their cycle of mutual repugnance that they can never separate. In his shrewd analysis of these marriages there is an underlying psychological insight which is one of Lever's greatest strengths.

These novels gain immeasurably from their anti-heroines. Without the

Sewells *Sir Brook Fossbrooke* might reasonably be assigned to a mere footnote in any assessment of Lever's work, with them the novel achieves considerable significance in any analysis of his importance as a writer of psychological realism. Within the tighter framework of *The Bramleighs of Bishop's Folly*, Marion's role is less vital than that of her predecessor, but she remains an intriguing study of self-possessed ambition, almost of monomania, created by sexist repression.

In discussing Lever's fascination with the theme of the 'outsider', Tony Bareham dwells on the absence in *Lord Kilgobbin* of any fully centralised hero or heroine. So far as a heroine does exist then she must be Nina Kostalergi. In her passion and in her ability to fascinate men and to bend them to her will, she reveals some of the allure of Lucy Sewell, while her cold-blooded calculation in becoming engaged to a man she cannot respect, reveals the cynicism of Marion Bramleigh. Like Marion and Lucy, Nina is deeply flawed and like them she undergoes very little development, though, unlike them, she experiences redemption – albeit of an uncertain kind. She enters the narrative having defied convention and parental authority by fleeing her father and travelling alone across half of Europe; she leaves it, set for a journey across the globe, having again flown in the face of convention, defying what little authority Mathew Kearney might be able to exert, and in the company of a wanted convict and rebel. It is a feature of Lever's anti-heroines that as a rule they fail to 'grow': their stories are in no way typical of the convention of the *bildungsroman* and there is an undeniable bleakness in this failure. Nina is as impetuous at the end as at the beginning of *Lord Kilgobbin*; Marion remains equally cold and committed to her plan for social advancement; only Lucy Sewell exhibits any advance in her self-knowledge or revision of her moral stance, for instance in her refusal to tamper with Baron Lendrick's will. Despite this apparent absence of development, however, these three women, for all their lack of the conventional qualities of the nineteenth century heroine, are some of the most dynamic of all Lever's characters, and in their strength of depiction and depth of analysis, implied rather than explicit though the analysis is, they deserve to be ranked among the finest female portraits of the period.

In her decision to elope with the Fenian head-centre, Daniel Donogan, Nina Kostalergi finds her salvation, ostensibly at least. In fact, Nina's character undergoes remarkably little development during the course of *Lord Kilgobbin* (1872) and she remains as much a prey to spontaneous whim at the novel's conclusion as at its commencement. In line with the overall despondency of the novel, her future away from Ireland remains as wrapped in doubt and obscurity as that of the other characters who linger within its shores.

7

LAST EFFORTS

– I –

In the last four years of his life, Lever produced what might reasonably be described as the very worst and the very best of his novels: *That Boy of Norcott's* and *Lord Kilgobbin*. The circumstances of his life at this period provide ample excuses for the weakness and lack of direction which mar the first of these works and, at the same time, render the contrastingly high calibre of the latter particularly remarkable. In March 1867, after nearly nine years as vice-consul in Spezzia, he was appointed to the post of Consul at Trieste, but climate, inaccessibility and lack of congenial society rapidly turned his initial delight at the promotion into outright disgust:

he accepted Trieste as a great boon, but found it 'one of the dreariest, dullest, and vulgarest of dens, without even that resource one had in Austria of yore – of a gentlemanlike class in the higher bureaucracy, and the soldiers in command – all was canting and communistic; he abhorred the place, and himself for coming to it.'[1]

His letters written during this period are filled with his hatred of the town and, touchingly, of his absolute horror at the thought of being buried there, calling the possibility 'a great aggravation to dying'.[2] The decline in his health was exacerbated by unalleviated financial anxieties and by growing concern over his wife's continuing illness. In such circumstances it is not surprising that *That Boy of Norcott's* should exhibit signs of careless and inattentive composition. Stevenson tells us that it was criticised for being 'perfunctory and improbable' and the accusations are difficult to counter, despite Lever's apparent conviction that the novel had been a great success with his London audience.[3]

However sympathetically one might view his personal circumstances, it proves impossible to formulate a plausible critical defence of the novel. With the almost palpable embarrassment typical of Victorian biographers at having to step outside their chosen vocabulary of praise, Fitzpatrick describes *That Boy of Norcott's* with unaccustomed severity:

> Irresolution in guidance marks the author's conduct of his hero; and its plot exhibits the defects so often noticed by his early censor, McGlashan, of being 'huddled up'.[4]

Here, though, we discover none of that youthful spontaneity and light-heartedness – to say nothing of inexperience – which did so much to compensate for the same defects in *Harry Lorrequer* and *Charles O'Malley*. Not that the opening passages present an altogether stark contrast to the obvious merits of the immediately preceding *The Bramleighs of Bishop's Folly*. Indeed, there are definite similarities in the narrative structure of the two novels, with the protagonists moving from affluence and rank, through poverty and social uncertainty, to exile on the Adriatic coast. There are also occasional glimpses of something quite promising in individual episodes within the novel. Sir Roger Norcott's catechism for his young son, for example, seems darkly reminiscent of Polonius's advice to Laertes:

> 'They've been preparing you for a travelling circus, while I wanted to make you a gentleman. Mind me now, sir, and don't expect that I ever repeat my orders to any one. What I say once I mean to be observed. Let your past life be entirely forgotten by you – a thing that had no reality; begin from this day – from this very room – a new existence, which is to have neither link nor tie to what has gone before it. The persons you will see here, their ways, their manners, their tone, will be examples for your imitation; copy them, not servilely, nor indiscriminately, but as you will find how their traits will blend with your own nature. Never tell an untruth, never accept an insult without redress, be slow about forming friendships and where you hate, hate thoroughly.'[5]

But while Laertes's adventures in France remain largely hidden from the audience, Lever clearly delineates Digby Norcott's corruption by his father's sycophantic and dissolute companions. Another of the occasional rays of originality and depth can be discovered when Sir Roger's strength in hatred is powerfully, though melodramatically, revealed through his decision to create in facsimile the room in which he proposed marriage to his now estranged and despised wife:

> The little room, about nine or ten feet in diameter, contained but a few straw-bottomed chairs, and a painted table on which a tea-service of common blue-ware stood. A Dutch clock was on a bracket at one side of the window, and a stuffed bird – a grouse, I believe – occupied another. A straight-backed old sofa, covered with a vulgar chintz, stood against the wall; an open book, with a broken fan in the leaves, to mark the place, lay on the sofa. The book was *Paul and Virginia*. A common sheet almanac was nailed against the wall, but over the printed columns

of the months a piece of white paper was pasted, on which, in large letters, was written, 'June 11, 18—. *Dies infausta.*' I started. I had read that date once before in my mother's prayer-book, and I had learned it was her marriage-day. As a ray of sunlight displays in an instant every object within its beam, I at once saw the meaning of every detail around me. These were the humble accessories of that modest home from which my dear mother was taken; these were the grim reminders of the time my father desired to perpetuate as an undying sorrow. I trembled to think what a nature I should soon be confronted with, and how terrible must be the temper of a man whose resentments asked for such aliment to maintain them![6]

In its revelation of a secret 'other' life, and of the past's intrusion into the present, the scene is strangely suggestive of Charlotte Bronte's *Jane Eyre*, though it occurs near the beginning of the novel and is denied both the centrality and dramatic impact of the discovery of Rochester's deranged spouse.

Bearing in mind Lever's accepted strengths and weaknesses, the obvious flaws and improbabilities in plot are not so surprising as the lack of convincing characterisation – although the failure to explain Digby's miraculous recovery from an apparently mortal illness in chapter eight is cavalier by even his own youthful standards. The characters introduced in the early portions of the novel are not remarkable, either for strength or weakness. They are credible but uninteresting: a damning enough judgement, perhaps, for a novelist with Lever's skills in characterisation. The two most promising individuals are Sir Roger and his mistress, Madame Cleremont; but while the former's hinted complexity is never fully realised, almost by an error of omission, Madame Cleremont is allowed to descend from an equivocal anti-heroism to two-dimensional villainy, providing a shallow and disappointing contrast to the depth of his previous anti-heroines. Introduced as an intelligent and talented woman, bound to a cold-hearted and brutal husband, she combines elements from the character of the passionate and unprincipled Lucy Sewell with those of the more cynical Marion Bramleigh. She bides her time and seemingly endures the snipes and innuendos of her husband, only occasionally allowing her mask to slip in front of the adoring Digby:

'It is well to remember that there are a number of excellent things one would like to be if they could afford them; but the truth is, Digby, the most costly of all things are virtues.'
'Oh, do not say that!' cried I eagerly.
'Yes, dear, I must say it. Monsieur Cleremont and I have always been very poor, and we never permitted ourselves these luxuries, any more than we kept a great house, and a fine equipage, and so we economise in our morals, as in our means, doing what rich folk might call little shabbinesses; but on the whole managing to live, and not unhappily either . . .'

'By this theory then, it is only rich people are good?'
'Not exactly. I would rather state it thus – the rich are as good as they like to be; the poor are as good as they're able.'⁷

As with Lucy Sewell, she is not simply a wronged ideal of Victorian womanhood. Rather, she is a clever woman willing to use her charms to influence others and whose position in the world has to a certain degree jaundiced her view of it, exaggerating a latent predatory instinct. While her views of the world may not be entirely sympathetic, the influences which have produced them and her ability to analyse both society and her ambiguous position within it, produce in the reader interest and, perhaps, empathy. As we might expect from Lever, the discovery that she has been mistress to Sir Roger and that their indifference to one another has been assumed, does not lead to outright condemnation. But at this point any attempt to engage the sympathies of his readers ends. Madame Cleremont appears next in the castle of an Hungarian count, shortly after Digby has been injured in a duel. Here, no effort is made to explain her rationale or to analyse her motivations. Described as a 'tigress', her ambition centres upon the desire to be accepted as Lady Norcott, no matter what the cost, and no matter who she must destroy to achieve her goal:

'So then,' cried she with a mocking laugh, 'you have got your courage up so far – you dare me! Be advised, however, and do not court such an unequal contest. I have but to choose in which of a score of ways I could crush you – do you mark me? crush you! You will not always be as lucky as you were this morning in the riding-school.'
'Great heaven!' cried I, 'was this then of your devising?'
'You begin to have a glimpse of whom you have to deal with? Go back to your room and reflect on that knowledge.'⁸

The revelation of her true character is not particularly shocking; earlier in the novel there are indications of her ambiguous ethical stance and of her vengefulness:

'I wonder how that woman stands it?' I once overheard Hotham say to Eccles; and the other replied,-
'I don't think she does stand it. I mistake her much if she is as forgiving as she looks.'⁹

What does surprise, however, is Lever's clumsy orchestration of the disclosure. He abandons all attempt at a subtle exploration of Madame Cleremont's motivations and instead thrusts her before the reader as a dyed-in-the-wool villainess, far removed from the multi-faceted delineation of both Lucy Sewell and Marion Bramleigh.

The weaknesses of *That Boy of Norcott's* are far more pronounced than any of its few strengths and, for once, the reader shares Lever's relief at concluding a novel. But the book does serve at least one useful function, that of yardstick by which to measure its successor, *Lord Kilgobbin*.

– II –

So far as any novel of Lever's has been described through superlatives, that novel is *Lord Kilgobbin*. Critical opinion unites in calling it his finest work, with its combination of strong characterisation, political observation and – of particular importance in any argument to counter the still prevalent perception of Lever as a lackey of the English establishment – outspoken condemnation of British misrule. A. Norman Jeffares has called it:

> the novel by which Lever should be judged. It is a despairing picture, of a decaying and discontented Anglo-Irish Ascendancy at the mercy of political unrest, angry terrorism and that English ineptitude, swinging between repression and appeasement, which he could not venerate.[10]

In dedicating the novel to his wife, whose death in April 1870 had devastated him, Lever stated 'The task that was once my joy and pride I have lived to find associated with my sorrow. It is not then without a cause I say – I hope this may be my last'. *Lord Kilgobbin* forms his swan-song, exploring many of his most serious concerns and fears. Although the tone is predominantly gloomy, however, there are also occasional flashes of light, of the mature and mellow humour to be found in *The Dodd Family Abroad*, and while he remained typically critical of his own work, stating that 'I have been tilting the cask so long that the dregs are coming out very muddy', most readers regard it as the distillation of a lifetime's observation, analysis and commentary.

As has been described elsewhere, in *Lord Kilgobbin* Lever's concern with the marginalised elements of society finds particularly fine expression. Furthermore, in his positioning of Kilgobbin Castle on the outskirts of the Bog of Allen, in the borderland between civilisation and desolation, we discover perhaps the finest example of his utilisation of architecture and geographic location to symbolise social ostracism. Uniquely, however, this representation is further heightened by the castle and the life of its occupants being endowed with an almost dreamlike quality:

> it would have been very difficult for any one to say ... wherein the quietude of even midnight was greater than that which prevailed there at noonday. Never, perhaps, were lives more completely still or monotonous than theirs. People who

derive no interests from the outer world, who know nothing of what goes on in life, gradually subside into a condition in which reflection takes the place of conversation, and lose all zest and all necessity for that small talk which serves, like the changes of a game, to while away time, and by the aid of which, if we do no more, we often delude the cares and worries of existence.[11]

Lever underpins the other-worldliness of Kilgobbin Castle with his treatment of its owner. Mathew Kearney is the scion of a noble and once wealthy Catholic family – a descendant of the ancient Irish landowners, whose claim to the land – like that of the O'Donoghues in his earlier novel – far outdates that of the Protestant Ascendancy. He is also a man out of step with the age in which he lives, an uncomfortable survivor of a previous era. Variations of Kearney, of his son Dick and daughter Kate, might have populated any one of Lever's earliest novels. But whereas in *Charles O'Malley* they would have been treated sympathetically, even indulgently, here their actions and motivations are examined far more critically. Rackrenting self-indulgence, the kind of hard-living and hard-drinking irresponsibility which has been masked with the term 'Irish hospitality', are now seen as destructive and almost effete. Kearney's nostalgia for this 'golden age' is sharply contrasted with his daughter's contempt for the same way of life:

The contrast between the sufferance under which his church existed at home and the honours and homage rendered to it abroad, were a fruitful stimulant to that disaffection he felt towards England, and would not unfrequently lead him away to long diatribes about penal laws and the many disabilities which had enslaved Ireland, and reduced himself, the descendant of a princely race, to the condition of a ruined gentleman.

To Kate these complainings were ever distasteful; she had but one philosophy, which was 'to bear up well,' and when not that, 'as well as you could.' She saw scores of things around her to be remedied, or, at least, bettered, by a little exertion, and not one which could be helped by a vain regret. For the loss of that old barbaric splendour and profuse luxury which her father mourned over, she had no regrets. She knew that these wasteful and profligate livers had done nothing for the people either in act or in example; that they were a selfish, worthless, self-indulgent race, caring for nothing but their pleasures, and making all their patriotism consist in a hate towards England.[12]

In the whole of Lever's works, there exists no more outright rejection of the kind of libertine philosophy which was tacitly sanctioned in the early novels. Furthermore, Kate's assessment of the old squirarchical lifestyle rings with downright certainty, while Kearney's has the warped and insubstantial nature of wistful nostalgia. By expressing his condemnation of the landowners' traditional profligacy through Kate, Lever lends the judgement a credibility denied to the opinions of her father. Novels such as *St Patrick's Eve* and *The Martins of Cro' Martin* form a valediction to the possibly apocryphal social contract between landlords and tenants. While the latter reveals a confirmed pessimism with regard to the possibility of any return to such a condition, there is still faith that it once existed and was truly beneficial. Here the pessimism has grown and the certainty that the squires were themselves largely responsible for their own fall from grace has broken down the barriers of Lever's reserve, opening the way for a forthright, though at times still nostalgic, reappraisal. Georg Lukacs's critique of Sir Walter Scott's treatment of aristocratic society and its failings can be applied with equal validity to Lever's work:

> he was able to portray objectively the ruination of past social formations, despite all his human sympathy for, and artistic sensitivity to, the splendid, heroic qualities which they contained. Objectively, in a large historical and artistic sense: he saw at one and the same time their outstanding qualities and the historical necessity of their decline.[13]

The strength of Lever's evolving commentary is that it seldom strays into self-contradiction because the process of evolution is a gradual one. At no point does he appear convinced that his belief system is absolute, rather it is prone to development and constant revision. In *Lord Kilgobbin*, as in all his other major novels, the opinions of no single character are permitted to predominate: Kearney's beliefs are juxtaposed with Kate's, Atlee's with Dick's, the Prince Kostalergi's with Lord Danesbury's. Of course, the danger inherent in this attempt to achieve a synthesis of opposing views is that Lever's works may sometimes appear to lack a strong central argument. On the other hand, a novelist who lacks the absolute certainty of dogma in his study of the condition of Ireland and in his proposals for resolution constitutes a refreshing exception to the established norm.

The ambiguity of Mathew Kearney's position – as the descendant of a family whose Catholic peerage dates to the days immediately following James II's defeat at the Boyne – and the uncertainty of his tenure, cascades down to the tenants of the estate whom Peter Gill, the steward, carefully keeps in 'quarantine against the outer world'.[14] Such is the steward's mastery of the estate's affairs, or rather such is his mastery over the confusion which he has himself created, that Kearney cannot face the prospect of his ever leaving his employ:

> As Gill was in perfect possession of her father's confidence, to oppose him in anything was a task of no mean difficulty; and the mere thought that the old fellow should feel offended and throw up his charge – a threat he had more than once half hinted – was a terror Kilgobbin could not have faced.[15]

Gill might be seen as an interesting development of Maria Edgeworth's manipulative and shrewd attorney, Jason Quirk, keeping both landlord and tenantry in a condition of permanent uncertainty and himself in a position of power – though, ultimately, it is not Kearney's estate which he masters but that of his eccentric and autocratic neighbour, Miss Betty O'Shea.

Despite the other-worldliness of Kilgobbin Castle, *Lord Kilgobbin* is not a fairy-tale. The subtitle 'A Tale of Ireland in our Own Time' plants it very firmly in the real world and perhaps one of the novel's greatest strengths lies in the contrast which it provides between the peculiar unreality of life within Kilgobbin and the harsh certainty of political developments and opinion outside the castle's precincts. The novel is Lever's most avowedly political work – practically every character becomes in some way involved, influenced or even dictated to by political events – A. Norman Jeffares has called it 'a continuation and culmination of the political attitudes of Lever's novels of the late 1850s and early to mid 1860s'.[16] The accuracy and frequency of the political commentary clearly evidence the failure of distance to prevent Lever from closely observing developments in Ireland. A political thread runs throughout the novel's course and is apparent even in its romantic interludes, often having a profound influence on the course of the individual lovers' suits. If Kilgobbin Castle in some ways stands apart from the everyday concerns of modern-day Ireland, in other ways it remains trapped by the ebb and flow of political events seething around its foundations. Constant reference is made, for instance, to the increasing dissatisfaction of the peasantry, despite the attempts of some landowners – such as Kate – to alleviate and improve their lot:

'Throw your eyes over that great expanse of dark bog . . . and bethink you how mere loneliness – desolation – needs a stout heart to bear it; how the simple fact that for long hours of a summer's day, or the longer hours of a winter's night, a lone woman has to watch and think of all the possible casualties lives of hardship and misery may impel men to. Do you imagine that she does not mark the growing discontent of the people? see their care-worn looks, dashed with sullen determination, and hear in their voices the rising of a hoarse defiance that was never heard before? Does she not well know that every kindness she has bestowed, every merciful act she has ministered, would weigh for nothing in the balance on the day that she will be arraigned as a landowner – the receiver of the poor man's rent!'[17]

Lord Kilgobbin is more closely tied to contemporary political events than any other of Lever's novels. These ties are reinforced by historical references, not merely to the semi-mythical tenant-landlord contract, but to previous evidence of unrest and of the incompetence of English rule:

to the oaths of the Whiteboys and Ribbonmen, for instance, or to the inherent uselessness of the famine-relief building projects of the 1840s. The latter are humorously highlighted through the confusion experienced by Walpole, a representative of the current administration, on the roads across the bog.[18]

So far as this sedentary novel can be said to include any 'adventurous' episode, then that episode must be the politically motivated night attack on Kilgobbin Castle. That this expansive novel contains only one such adventure, and the fact that it forms the core of the political commentary and is returned to periodically throughout the length of the work, form a stark contrast to the adventure-bestrewn early novels. Here, the lives of the characters are not full of excitement, they muddle along as best they can and when a disturbance occurs its effects are not quickly and dramatically superseded by the impact of another; instead, they are gradually woven into the continuing course of everyday events. This realism is reinforced by the advent and subsequent departure of Kearney's niece, Nina Kostalergi:

> Kilgobbin Castle fell back to the ways in which our first chapter found it, and other interests – especially those of Kate's approaching marriage – soon effaced the memory of Nina's flight and runaway match. By that happy law by which the waves of events follow and obliterate each other, the present glided back into the past, and the past faded till its colours grew uncertain.[19]

No melodramatic catharsis takes place and the thread of Nina's story is subsumed in the weft and warp of Kilgobbin's history, in the same way in which the relatively recent attack of the Whiteboys has become the stuff of legend, brought out and dusted off to be used in comparison with Kate's late defence.[20] This subsumption provides a practical demonstration of Lukacs's theory that 'a collision in a novel does not have to be represented in its highest and sharpest form and then violently resolved'.[21]

Lord Kilgobbin boldly underlines the reality that no matter how far removed from political interests an individual may be, the social and political climate of Ireland can endow their most natural and instinctive reaction with a political dimension. It is no accident that one of the key players in the novel's single adventure is Kate Kearney, the least political of all the characters. Kate's one motivation is the defence of her family home and her predominant emotion contempt for the men who will only dare attack the Castle when her father is known to be away on business. Once the incident reaches the press, however, very different reasons are ascribed to her actions. Nationalist and loyalist are equally wide of the mark. The former paints her actions in the darkest hue:

'our contemporaries,' it began, 'are recounting with more than their wonted eloquence the injuries inflicted on three poor labouring-men, who, in their ignorance of the locality, had the temerity to ask for alms at Kilgobbin Castle yesterday evening, and were ignominiously driven away from the door by a young lady, whose benevolence was administered through a blunderbuss.'[22]

The latter eulogises not only the heroine herself, but also the whole of the ramshackle Kilgobbin estate and its management:

'If it was our wish to exhibit to a stranger the picture of an Irish estate in which all the blessings of good management, intelligence, kindliness, and Christian charity were displayed; to show him a property where the well-being of landlord and tenant were inextricably united, where the condition of the people, their dress, their homes, their food, and their daily comforts could stand comparison with the most favoured English county, we should point to the Kearney estate of Kilgobbin.'[23]

The partisans of each dogma manipulate the truth to suit their needs and Kate becomes nothing more than a pawn in their game: an oppressive tartar to one, to the other the beneficent ruler of a pre-lapsarian Eden.

The corruption of the press and its partisan failure to attempt any real analysis of events are highlighted through the career of Joe Atlee. 'The son of a Presbyterian minister in the north of Ireland', the impecunious and mercenary Atlee writes for the mouthpieces of both sides of the political divide:

These journals were of every political tint, from emerald green to the deepest orange; and, indeed, between two of them – the *Tipperary Pike* and the *Boyne Water*, hailing from Carrickfergus – there was a controversy of such violence and intemperance of language, that it was a curiosity to see the two papers on the same table: the fact being capable of explanation, that they were both written by Joe Atlee.[24]

In some ways the most sympathetic of the male characters – with his wit, repartee and genuine intelligence – he is also the object of Lever's most uncompromising criticism as representing the cold-blooded cynicism of a deliberate failure to utilise his obvious abilities for anything other than selfish ends. Atlee forms the focus for some of the novel's most humorous incidents but as the story develops, Lever's attitude towards him hardens until, in the closing chapters, he is made to seem absurd and even pathetic in the excesses of his over-weaning self-confidence. Despite his flaws, however, and his deplorable willingness to prostitute his talents to the highest bidder, Atlee's proven intelligence lends credibility to many of his pronouncements and it is through him that Lever makes some of his most critical comments on the condition of Ireland and on English mal-administration. Although, for money and for amusement, he will write for journals of the 'deepest orange', Atlee's opinions are clearly Nationalist – though their most acute expression is to be found not in his journalism but in his conversation and in his anonymous penny-ballads:

> Is there anything more we can fight or can hate for?
>   The 'drop' and the famine have made our ranks thin.
> In the name of endurance, then, what do we wait for?
>   Will nobody give us the word to begin?
>
> Some brothers have left us in sadness and sorrow,
>   In despair of the cause they had sworn to win;
> They owned they were sick of that cry of 'to-morrow;'
>   Not a man would believe that we meant to begin.[25]

There is a kernel of Nationalist faith in Atlee, and in his response to the arrogance of the Englishman, Walpole, a bitterness and anguish seldom apparent in Lever's other works. But these emotions are subjugated to his 'snobbery' and to his desire to get on in the world, resulting finally in his becoming the aide of Lord Danesbury and in his habitation of the hollow position of servant to a regime which he despises. Atlee serves another important function, acting as a link between the scenes set in Ireland, in Wales and in Greece and Constantinople. Even before he enters the employ of Lord Danesbury and undertakes a diplomatic mission, his familiarity with European events and history allows him to draw comparisons:

'And do you know anything on the subject?'
'About as much as the present Cabinet does of Ireland. I know all the claptraps; the grand traditions that have sunk down into a present barbarism – of course, through ill government; the noble instincts depraved by gross ill-usage; I know the inherent love of freedom we cherish, which makes men resent rents as well as laws, and teaches that taxes are as great a tyranny as the rights of property.'
'And do the Greeks take this view of it?'
'Of course they do; and it was in experimenting on them that your great Ministers learned how to deal with Ireland. There was but one step from Thebes to Tipperary. Corfu was 'pacified' – that's the phrase for it – by abolishing the landlords.'[26]

In comparisons and references like these, as well as in the actual transfer of the action to Constantinople and Athens, the spaciousness identified by A. Norman Jeffares can be found,[27] and Lever's importance as a Europeanised critic of Irish life recognised.

If Atlee's role is to some degree a reactive one, providing a vocal critique of English rule, then the mouthpiece of the administration is Cecil Walpole, cousin and private secretary to the new viceroy, Lord

Danesbury. Walpole articulates the beliefs and principles of government and, even without the commentary of Atlee, he succeeds in condemning both himself and the administration with his own words and actions. In his introduction to the reader there is an interesting and deliberate throwback to the kind of 'English or Anglofied-Irish tourist in Ireland' novels which were so prevalent in the early years of the century and, indeed, to Lever's own early work, *Jack Hinton*. The difference between these early examples of the new-born Anglo-Irish novel and *Lord Kilgobbin*, however, lies in the stark lack of optimism in the latter. Whereas in novels such as Maria Edgeworth's *Ennui* (1809) and *The Absentee* (1812), the heroes gradually accumulate knowledge of the country and exchange prejudice for understanding and sympathy, no such development occurs in Walpole. His insularity remains uninvaded and his contempt for all things Irish unaltered and readily expressed from first to last:

The Ireland of wits, dramatists, and romance-writers was a conventional thing, and bore no resemblance whatsoever to the rain-soaked, dreary-looking, depressed reality. 'These Irish, they are odd without being droll, just as they are poor without being picturesque; but of all the delusions we nourish about them, there is none so thoroughly absurd as to call them dangerous!'[28]

Having been subjected to Walpole's ignorance and arrogant dismissiveness, the reader feels a distinct though grim satisfaction in finding him, a few chapters further on, prostrated with an arm shattered by the bullet of a Fenian. The resilience of Walpole's prejudice becomes in some ways the symbol of British obtuseness; neither he nor the administration appears to learn from their ever growing burden of experience. Still recovering from his wound, we find him admonishing the Irish Atlee:

'Above all things, let me warn you against a favourite blunder of your countrymen. Don't endeavour to explain peculiarities of action in this country by singularities of race or origin; don't try to make out that there are special points of view held that are unknown on the other side of the channel, or that there are other differences between the two peoples, except such as more rags and greater wretchedness produce. We have got over that very venerable and time-honoured blunder, and do not endeavour to revive it.'[29]

While Lever's attitude toward Walpole is a condemnatory one, as in the case of Atlee, his intelligence and knowledge of the world at large are sufficient to make him a useful organ for the expression of certain truths. Both men are self-serving and essentially cold-hearted, but while Atlee voices the bitterness and national resentment of so many young Irishmen, Walpole's attitude toward Ireland is clearly intended to have an application which is broader than the limitations of his own small nature, and his knowledge and understanding of the government's practices is seen to be based upon observation rather than fancy. This consistency of belief is underpinned by Lord Danesbury's views on the condition of Ireland and the history of English rule:

'An extra blunder in the conduct of Irish affairs is only like an additional mask in a fancy ball – the whole thing is motley; and asking for consistency would be like requesting the company to behave like arch-deacons.'[30]

As in so many of his novels, Lever allows his characters to stand and fall by their own actions and pronouncements. Seldom intruding his own voice into the narrative, he was aware of the risk in allowing his creations too much autonomy, and admitted that 'there is scarcely a character in the book has not got away from me and set up on his own account'.[31] Whether deliberate or the product of his characters' independence, the fact remains that the prevailing political tone of *Lord Kilgobbin* is anti-British.

Of course, the most compelling condemnation of the vice-royalty comes from Daniel Donogan, a character loosely based upon the Fenian head-centre, Jeremiah O'Donovan Rossa (1831-1915). A. Norman Jeffares states that:

the ambitious young men in *Lord Kilgobbin* are sharply, calculatingly intent upon achieving successful careers for themselves.[32]

Donogan represents the exception to this rule and his radicalism, passion and commitment to his beliefs come as a breath of fresh air after the cynicism and self-serving of Atlee, Walpole and, to a lesser degree, Dick Kearney. As has been analysed elsewhere, Lever's primary concern throughout his novels lay with the classes of society which he most understood and with whom he had the greatest familiarity: the upper-middle classes. Donogan belongs to this class, being both a landowner and a trained physician. Lever's decision to deliver his most bitter denunciation of English rule through such a medium lends his words conviction and credibility. Donogan's references to the government's deliberate extermination of the Irish language has a particular resonance and reflects the Fenian concern, from the 1850s onwards, for the survival of the Irish language:

'In one thing, your Greeks have an immense advantage over us here. In your popular songs you could employ your own language, and deal with your own wrongs in the accents that became them. We had to take the tongue of the conqueror, which was as little suited to our tradition as to our feelings, and travestied both. Only imagine the Greek vaunting his triumphs or bewailing his defeats in Turkish!'[33]

Had Lever chosen to make such pronouncements through the spokesman of any other class, the peasantry for instance, the words would have lost some of their power and naturalism. As James M. Cahalan has pointed out, 'Politically, this novel shows just how far Lever had moved from his Ascendancy stereotype, his opposition to British policies deepening enough to allow himself to make a Fenian his hero'.[34] It would be a mistake, however, to believe that this broadening of sympathies went so far as to become an actual inversion of his original political stance. Another of Donogan's statements, on the utility of the British parliamentary system to the Fenian movement, reads very much like an elegy for many of those institutions, which as a Protestant and a Tory, Lever would have held dear:

'we begin to perceive that to assault that heavy bastion of Saxon intolerance, we must have spies in the enemy's fortress, and for this we send in so many members to the Whig Party. There are scores of men who will aid us by their vote who would not risk a bone in our cause. Theirs is a sort of subacute patriotism; but it has its use. It smashes an Established Church, breaks down Protestant ascendancy, destroys the prestige of landed property, and will in time abrogate entail and primogeniture, and many another fine thing; and in this way it clears the ground for our operations, just as soldiers fell trees and level houses lest they interfere with the range of heavy artillery.'[35]

Whether or not Lever might agree with Donogan's actions and motivations, the fact remains that by making the Fenian the most sympathetic and principled of the male characters, his views are rendered worthy of consideration. This attitude is representative of the synthesis of political opinion apparent throughout the novel and it is further reinforced by the surprising accord reached by Kearney and the Tory magistrate, Flood, the representatives of the traditional political divide:

'The finest peasantry have a taste for kicking with strong brogues on them, Mr Kearney, that cannot be equalled.'
'I wish with all my heart they'd kick the English out of Ireland!' cried Kearney, with a savage energy.
'Faith! if they go on governing us in the present fashion, I do not say I'll make any great objection . . .'
'I'm sick of them all, Whigs and Tories,' said Kearney.
'Is not every Irish gentleman sick of them, Mr Kearney? Ain't you sick of being cheated and cajoled, and ain't we sick of being cheated and insulted? They seek to conciliate you by outraging us. Don't you think we could settle our own differences better amongst ourselves . . . Now, Mr Kearney, what if we all took to "pulling together?"'[36]

There is in *Lord Kilgobbin*, no character whose opinion we are expected to take seriously whose words or actions support the continuance of English rule in Ireland. Admittedly, Kate does make a statement of personal support for the English administration, albeit in the midst of a swingeing criticism of the same institution:

'You might have heard far more of his recklessness, if Donogan cared to tell of it,' said Kate, with irritation. 'It is not English squadrons and batteries he is called alone to face, he has to meet English gold, that tempts poverty, and English corruption, that begets treachery and betrayal. The one stronghold of the Saxon here is the informer, and mind, I, who tell this, am no rebel. I would rather live under English law, if English law would not ignore Irish feeling.'[37]

It is absolutely typical of the mature Lever that the one comment made in support of a continuance of the vice-royalty is made with a proviso which the pessimism of the novel as a whole, and its examination of English administrative practices in particular, renders impossible of compliance.

In his early novel, *The O'Donoghue*, Lever was handicapped by an obvious ignorance of anything beyond the most commonly understood details of the movement of the United Irishmen – a knowledge of which would have lifted this important work from the rank of *bildungsroman* to the level of a true historical novel. A contrasting strength of *Lord Kilgobbin* is his familiarity with the political and social developments in Ireland during the years immediately preceding the writing of the novel, a familiarity clearly evidenced in his correspondence:

The Whigs would like to blend up Fenianism and agrarian crime. Now they are not to be so confounded. The National party is anti-English, rebel, violent, cruel, anything you like, but the men who shoot the landlords are not the Fenians![38]

His ability to tie these events to the formulation of the opinions and beliefs of his characters is pronounced. Fenianism is not relegated to the subsidiary role of 'background colour'; instead, he makes a real attempt to analyse the motivation of the movement's leaders. The description is not altogether a complimentary one, dwelling upon the movement's violence and cynicism and its unforgiving attitude towards any who questioned its tactics. Possibly, Lever's sympathy for Donogan, and his own distrust of Fenianism led him to divorce one from the other. By the end of the novel, and as a direct result of his devotion to Nina, Donogan has separated himself from the Fenian hierarchy.

Occasional reference is made to the disestablishment of the Church of Ireland, but even more regularly adverted to is the contentious legislation which passed to the tenantry supremacy in the question of land rights. R.F. Foster describes the process:

From the 1860s William Ewart Gladstone (an ex-Peelite, now leading the liberals) attempted a series of political measures (not necessarily inter-connected, for all his retrospective claims). The 1869 Act disestablishing the Church of Ireland (although on very favourable terms) was one response; another was the 1870 Land Act, giving the right of compensation to evicted tenants for expenditure made on their holdings, and applying the supposed 'Ulster custom' of tenant right all over Ireland. These measures were inadequate responses to the problems of alienation and poverty which they were designed to meet; but they were of symbolic importance in implying the end of Ascendancy of Protestants and landlords, many of whom angrily interpreted Gladstonian legislation in just these terms.[39]

An inveterate opponent of Gladstone's measures – he admitted to John Blackwood that, 'Every fresh speech of Gladstone gives me a fresh seizure'[40] – most of Lever's mature novels reveal an inherent recognition of the inevitability of such reform in the face of generations of Ascendancy incompetence and short-sighted self-indulgence. For this reason, the many references to the causes and results of the Gladstonian legislation are not, perhaps, as acerbic as one might expect. Instead, although the impact of the land laws is described as pernicious, there is, again, the quality of resignation to the inevitable:

'Now here's two things that are about to take place: one is the same as done, for it's all ready prepared, – the taking of the landlord's right, and making the State determine what rent the tenant shall pay, and how long his tenure will be. The second won't come for two sessions after, but it will be law all the same. There's to be no primogeniture class at all, no entail on land, but a subdivision, like in America and, I believe, in France.'

'I don't believe it, sir. These would amount to a revolution.'

'Well, and why not? Ain't we always going through a sort of mild revolution? What's parliamentary government but revolution, weakened, if you like, like watered grog, but the spirit is there all the same. Don't fancy that, because you give it a hard name you can destroy it.'[41]

A. Norman Jeffares has accurately described *Lord Kilgobbin* as 'a despairing picture'. Although there are humorous episodes – most noticeably in the descriptions of Kearney's troubled relationship with Miss Betty – the hopefulness expressed in *St Patrick's Eve* regarding a possible return to the halcyon days of tenant-landlord co-operation, and the half-wistful, half-bleak attitude of *The Martins of Cro' Martin* have been superseded by a dark pessimism, which permits no possibility of resolution to the 'Irish Question'. While Sir Walter Scott found 'in English history the consolation that the most violent vicissitudes of class struggle have always finally calmed down into a glorious "middle way"',[42] Irish history permitted no such optimism to Lever. Nina and Donogan are allowed a ray of light, in their shared future in America, but if they achieve happiness it will not be on Irish soil; and while Kate and Gorman O'Shea bask in the glow of their forthcoming marriage,

Donogan's comments on the unforgiving antagonism of the Nationalists leaves little hope that their tenure of O'Shea's Barn will remain undisturbed. *Lord Kilgobbin* offers no remedy and, in a way, no conclusion at all; as the closing lines of the novel reveal, what has been described is, in essence, an episode. There has been no alleviation of the unrest referred to from the earliest pages; Kearney's position remains as ambiguous as before; the ignorance and incomprehension between English and Irish are as strong as ever; and the antagonism created by Kate's defence of the Castle promises further ill-feeling and probable reprisals. As *Harry Lorrequer* might be thought of as the capturing of an episodic snap-shot of its hero's adventurous life, *Lord Kilgobbin* is presented deliberately as but a portion of the dark tapestry of Irish existence.

Against the certainty of Irish politics and social upheaval, *Lord Kilgobbin* can be seen as Lever's fullest examination of the insubstantial – of the unreality of things. Nothing is quite what it seems: the position of Kilgobbin Castle in the borderland between desolation and cultivation; the social ambiguity of Mathew Kearney's standing, and the uncertainty of his tenure; the self-serving and shallow friendships not only of Dick Kearney and Joe Atlee but also of Walpole and Lockwood; the cynical betrothal of Walpole and Lady Maude; and the shadowy presence and influence of the Prince Kostalergi. Between the beginning of his writing career and its end, the emphasis of Lever's novels had been almost totally inverted. In *Harry Lorrequer*, only the escapades of the hero have substance and loom large against the backdrop of an Ireland hardly tangible and possessed of absolutely no political identity. By the time of *Lord Kilgobbin*, however, the political reality of the country predominates and the characters who move across its face – astutely drawn though they are – are almost ghostly when measured by the impact of their actions upon the juggernaut of history.

NOTES

TITLE PAGE

1 Charles Lever, *Cornelius O'Dowd*. (Edinburgh and London: William Blackwood and Sons, 1864) First Series, p.v

FOREWORD BY BENEDICT KIELY

1 Charles Lever, *The Daltons*. (London: Downey and Co., 1898) I, p.229
2 Charles Lever, *Jack Hinton, the Guardsman*. (London: Downey and Co., 1897) pp.351–352

INTRODUCTION
WRITING ON THE MARGINS

1 Charles Lever, *Confessions of Harry Lorrequer*. (Dublin: William Curry, 1839) Advertisements
2 J.A. Sutherland, *Victorian Novelists and Publishers*. (Chicago: University of Chicago Press, 1976) pp.162–163
3 *Ibid*. p.164
4 Lever, *Harry Lorrequer*. (London: George Routledge and Sons, n.d.) pp.x–xi
5 Sutherland, *Victorian Novelists and Publishers*, pp.163–164
6 Thomas Kilroy, introduction to Joseph Sheridan Le Fanu, *The House by the Churchyard*. (Belfast: The Appletree Press, 1992) p.xii
7 Quoted by R.F. Foster, *Paddy and Mr Punch*. (London: Penguin, 1995) p.76
8 Tony Bareham (ed.), *Charles Lever: New Evaluations*. (Gerrards Cross: Colin Smythe, 1991) pp.18–22
9 Georg Lukacs, *The Historical Novel*. (London: Penguin, 1981) pp.59–60
10 James M. Cahalan, *The Irish Novel*. (Dublin: Gill and Macmillan, 1988) p.67
11 R.F. Foster, *Paddy and Mr Punch*. p.68
12 Lever, *The Martins of Cro' Martin*. (London: George Routledge and Sons, n.d.) I, p.163
13 Lever, *The O'Donoghue*. (London: George Routledge and Sons, n.d.) p.152
14 Foster, *Paddy and Mr Punch*. p.xiii
15 Tony Bareham (ed.), *Charles Lever: New Evaluations*. p.96

16 *Ibid.* p.96
17 G.B. Shaw, quoted by R.F. Foster, *Paddy and Mr Punch.* p.291
18 Quoted by Lionel Stevenson, *Dr Quicksilver – the Life of Charles Lever.* (London: Chapman and Hall, 1939) p.218
19 A. Norman Jeffares, introduction to Lever, *Lord Kilgobbin.* (Belfast: The Appletree Press, 1992) p.ix
20 Foster, *Paddy and Mr Punch.* p.xii
21 A. Norman Jeffares, *Anglo-Irish Literature.* (Dublin: Gill and Macmillan, 1982) p.1
22 Quoted by Barry Sloan, *Pioneers of Anglo-Irish Fiction 1800–1850.* (Gerrards Cross: Colin Smythe, 1986) p.191
23 Anthony Trollope, *Autobiography.* (Edinburgh and London: William Blackwood and Sons, 1883) II, pp.74–75
24 George Saintsbury, *Nineteenth Century Literature.* (London: Macmillan and Co., 1896) p.158
25 Declan Kiberd in: R.F. Foster (ed.), *The Oxford Illustrated History of Ireland.* (Oxford: Oxford University Press, 1989) p.307
26 Chris Morash, *The Arts Show.* (Dublin: RTE, February 1994)
27 Quoted by Foster, *Paddy and Mr Punch.* p.305
28 *Ibid.* p.xvi
29 *Ibid.* p.26
30 *Ibid.* p.28
31 *Ibid.* p.29
32 Quoted by Declan Kiberd in: Foster (ed.), *Illustrated History of Ireland.* p.307
33 Lever, *The Martins of Cro' Martin.* II, p.342
34 Quoted by W.J. Fitzpatrick, *The Life of Charles Lever.* (London: Ward, Lock and Co., 1884) p.110
35 Catherine Peters, *Thackeray's Universe: Shifting Worlds of Imagination and Reality.* (London: Faber and Faber, 1987) p.106
36 Lever, *Charles O'Malley.* (London: George Routledge and Sons, n.d.) p.viii
37 Chris Morash in: Otto Rauchbauer (ed.), *Ancestral Voices: The Big House in Anglo-Irish Literature.* (Hildesheim: Geor Olms Verlag, 1992) p.73
38 Stevenson, *Dr Quicksilver.* p.277
39 Bill Rodgers in: Bareham (ed.), *Charles Lever: New Evaluations.* p.72
40 Bareham (ed.), *Charles Lever: New Evaluations.* p.107
41 Charles Lever, *The Bramleighs of Bishop's Folly.* (London: The Cornhill Magazine, June 1867) p.643
42 Charles Lever, *Sir Brook Fossbrooke.* (London: George Routledge and Sons, n.d.) pp.339–340
43 Chris Morash in: Bareham (ed.), *Charles Lever: New Evaluations.* p.86
44 A. Norman Jeffares in: Bareham (ed.), *Charles Lever: New Evaluations.* pp.18–21
45 Foster, *Paddy and Mr Punch.* p.27
46 Cahalan, *The Irish Novel.* p.64
47 Charles Lever, *That Boy of Norcott's.* (London: George Routledge and Sons, n.d.) p.110
48 Lever, *Lord Kilgobbin.* (Belfast: The Appletree Press, 1992) p.128
49 Sutherland, *Victorian Novelists and Publishers.* p.21

Notes

50 Bareham (ed.), *Charles Lever: New Evaluations*. p.3
51 Lever, *Harry Lorrequer*. pp.vii–viii
52 Sutherland, *Victorian Novelists and Publishers*. p.172
53 Quoted by Cahalan, *The Irish Novel*. pp.14–15
54 *Ibid*. p.15
55 Trollope, *Autobiography*. II, p.75
56 Edmund Downey, *Charles Lever: His Life in His Letters*. (Edinburgh and London: William Blackwood and Sons, 1906) I, p.182
57 *Ibid*. I, p.182
58 *Ibid*. I, p.204
59 Charles Lever, *The Fortunes of Glencore*. (London: George Routledge and Sons, n.d.) p.vi
60 Lever, *Harry Lorrequer*. p.v
61 Bareham (ed.), *Charles Lever: New Evaluations*. p.2

CHAPTER ONE

THE NOVELS OF DR QUICKSILVER

1 Carleton's review appeared in *The Nation*, October 1843
2 W.B.Yeats, 'Popular Ballad Poetry of Ireland', in *The Leisure Hour*, November 1889
3 James M. Cahalan, *The Irish Novel, A Critical History*. (Dublin: Gill and Macmillan, 1988) p.67
4 Charles Lever, *The Confessions of Harry Lorrequer*. (London: Routledge and Sons, n.d.) p.v
5 Quoted by Tony Bareham (ed.), *Charles Lever: New Evaluations*. (Gerrards Cross: Colin Smythe, 1991) p.3
6 Barry Sloan, *The Pioneers of Anglo-Irish Fiction 1800–1850*. (Gerrards Cross: Colin Smythe, 1986) p.193
7 Edmund Downey, *Charles Lever: His Life in His Letters*. (Edinburgh and London: William Blackwood and Sons, 1906) I, p.186
8 Cahalan, *The Irish Novel*. p.67
9 Lever, *Harry Lorrequer*. pp.v–vi
10 Downey, *Charles Lever: His Life in His Letters*. I, p.186
11 *Ibid*. p.101
12 *Ibid*. p.102
13 *Ibid*. p.305
14 *Ibid*. pp.5–6
15 Cahalan, *The Irish Novel*. p.15
16 Sloan, *The Pioneers of Anglo-Irish Fiction*. p.194
17 Lever, *Charles O'Malley*. (London: Routledge and Sons, n.d.) p.vii
18 *Ibid*. p.viii
19 Cahalan, *The Irish Novel*. p.68
20 W.J. Fitzpatrick, *The Life of Charles Lever*. (London: Ward, Lock, & Co., 1884) p.140
21 Lever, *Charles O'Malley*. I, p.122
22 Cahalan, *The Irish Novel*. p.68

23 Lever, *Charles O'Malley.* I, p.106
24 Henry Cockton, *Valentine Vox, the Ventriloquist* (London: Herbert Jenkins, n.d.) p.92
25 Lever, *Harry Lorrequer.* p.47
26 Lever, *Charles O'Malley.* I, pp.52–53
27 Bareham, *Charles Lever: New Evaluations.* p.112
28 Lever, *Charles O'Malley.* II, p.324
29 Lionel Stevenson, *Dr Quicksilver: the life of Charles Lever.* (London: Chapman and Hall, 1939) pp.75–6
30 Lever, *Charles O'Malley.* I, p.vii
31 Fitzpatrick, *The Life of Charles Lever.* p.155
32 Georg Lukacs, *The Historical Novel.* (London: Penguin Books, 1962) pp.44–45
33 Lever, *Charles O'Malley.* II, pp.269–270
34 Quoted by Anthony Livesy: *The Penguin Atlas of WWI.* (London: Penguin, 1994) p.126
35 Lever, *Charles O'Malley.* II, p.451
36 Stevenson, *Dr Quicksilver.* p.197
37 Fitzpatrick, *The Life of Charles Lever.* p.140
38 Lever, *Charles O'Malley.* I, p.xv
39 *Ibid.* I, p.79
40 *Ibid.* II, pp.216–217
41 Downey, *Charles Lever: His Life in His Letters.* I, pp.186–187
42 Lorna Reynolds, 'A Tale of Love and War' in: Bareham (ed.), *Charles Lever: New Evaluations.* p.38
43 *Ibid.* p.48
44 Lever, *Charles O'Malley.* II, p.328
45 Sloan, *The Pioneers of Anglo-Irish Fiction.* p.192
46 Bareham, *Charles Lever: New Evaluations.* p.48
47 Fitzpatrick, *The Life of Charles Lever.* p.129
48 *Ibid.* p.150
49 Stevenson, *Dr Quicksilver.* p.83
50 *Ibid.* p.79
51 *Ibid.* p.76
52 *Ibid.* p.76

CHAPTER TWO

A YEAR OF GROWTH

1 Barry Sloan, *The Pioneers of Anglo-Irish Fiction 1800–1850.* (Gerrards Cross: Colin Smythe, 1986) p.205
2 Charles Lever, *The O'Donoghue, a Tale of Ireland Fifty Years Ago.* (London: George Routledge and Sons, n.d.) p.146
3 *Ibid.* pp.130–131
4 Sloan, *The Pioneers of Anglo-Irish Fiction.* p.206
5 Lever, *The O'Donoghue.* p.vii

Notes

6 *Ibid.* p.37
7 *Ibid.* pp.4–5
8 *Ibid.* p.5
9 R.F. Foster (ed.), *The Oxford Illustrated History of Ireland.* (Oxford: Oxford University Press, 1989) p.174
10 Lever, *The O'Donoghue.* p.191
11 *Ibid.* p.199
12 *Ibid.* p.338
13 *Ibid.* p.381
14 *Ibid.* p.382
15 *Ibid.* p.476
16 Quoted by James M. Cahalan, *The Irish Novel.* (Dublin: Gill and Macmillan, 1988) p.64
17 A. Norman Jeffares, introduction to: Lever, *Lord Kilgobbin.* (Belfast: Appletree Press, 1992) p.ix
18 *Ibid.* p.ix
19 Lever, *The O'Donoghue.* pp.370–371
20 Charles Lever, *Lord Kilgobbin.* (Belfast: Appletree Press, 1992) p.124
21 Chris Morash in: Tony Bareham (ed.), *Charles Lever: New Evaluations.* (Gerrards Cross: Colin Smythe, 1991) p.87
22 Lever, *The O'Donoghue.* p.17
23 Lever, *Lord Kilgobbin.* p.3
24 Lever, *The O'Donoghue.* p.230
25 Lever, *Lord Kilgobbin.* p.179
26 Quoted by Lionel Stevenson, *Dr Quicksilver – the Life of Charles Lever.* (London: Chapman and Hall, 1939) pp.142–143
27 *Ibid.* p.149
28 Lever, *Charles O'Malley.* (London: Routledge and Sons, n.d.) p.v
29 In 1833 Lever sent to London, via a Dublin bookseller, his story entitled 'The Black Mask'. Having been advised by his agent that the piece had not been published but unable to secure its return, the novelist rewrote it from memory and contributed it to *The Dublin University Magazine.* In fact the story had been published in London, appearing as a 'translation' in *The Storyteller.* Carleton's accusation of plagiarism was based upon his having seen this first version – the publication of which its author was entirely ignorant.
30 Quoted by Stevenson, *Dr Quicksilver.* p.54
31 Lever, *Charles O'Malley.* p.v
32 Charles Lever, *St Patrick's Eve.* (London: Chapman and Hall, 1845) p.i (dedication)
33 Charles Lever, *St Patrick's Eve*, appearing in the same volume as *That Boy of Norcott's.* (London: Routledge and Sons, n.d.) p.435
34 Richard Haslam in: Bareham (ed.), *Charles Lever: New Evaluations* p.77
35 Quoted by Stevenson, *Dr Quicksilver.* p.138
36 R.F. Foster, *Modern Ireland, 1600–1972.* (London: Penguin, 1988) p.179
37 Edmund Downey, *Charles Lever: His Life in His Letters.* (Edinburgh and London: William Blackwood and Sons, 1906) I, p.191

CHAPTER THREE
AN INIQUITOUS ACT

1. Lionel Stevenson, *Dr Quicksilver – the Life of Charles Lever*. (London: Chapman and Hall, 1939) p.153
2. The last of Lever's novels to be published by Chapman and Hall was *Luttrell of Arran* (London: 1865)
3. J.A. Sutherland, *Victorian Novelists and Publishers*. (Chicago: University of Chicago Press, 1976) pp.162–3
4. R.F. Foster, *Modern Ireland, 1600–1972*. (London: Penguin, 1989) p.282
5. *Ibid.* p.282
6. *Ibid.* p.289
7. Edmund Downey, *Charles Lever: His Life in His Letters*. (Edinburgh and London: William Blackwood and Sons, 1906) I, p.200
8. Charles Lever, *The Knight of Gwynne*. (London: Downey and Co., 1897) I, pp.188–189
9. Foster, *Modern Ireland*. p.284
10. Lever, *The Knight of Gwynne*. I, pp.384–5
11. *Ibid.* I, p.388
12. *Ibid.* I, p.140
13. *Ibid.* II, p.103
14. *Ibid.* II, p.174
15. Stevenson, *Dr Quicksilver*. p.110
16. Lever, *The Knight of Gwynne* II, p.65
17. *Ibid.* II, p.72
18. *Ibid.* II, pp.362–363
19. *Ibid.* I, p.100
20. *Ibid.* I, p.352
21. *Ibid.* I, p.232
22. *Ibid.* I, pp.90–91
23. *Ibid.* I, pp.351–352
24. *Ibid.* I, p.293
25. Sutherland, *Victorian Novelists and Publishers*. p.163
26. W.J. Fitzpatrick, *The Life of Charles Lever*. (London: Ward, Lock and Co., 1884) p.257
27. Stevenson, *Dr Quicksilver*. p.152
28. See: Introduction, note 58

CHAPTER FOUR
THE DOUBLE-SIDED COIN

1. Lionel Stevenson, *Dr Quicksilver – the Life of Charles Lever*. (London: Chapman and Hall, 1939) p.197
2. Edmund Downey, *Charles Lever: His Life in His Letters*. (Edinburgh: William Blackwood and Sons, 1906) vol. I, p.388
3. *Ibid.* p.386–7

Notes

4. Stevenson, *Dr Quicksilver*. p.197
5. W.J. Fitzpatrick, *The Life of Charles Lever*. (London: Ward, Lock and Co., 1884) p.295
6. *Ibid.* p.295
7. Downey, *Charles Lever: His Life in His Letters*. I, p.388
8. Charles Lever, *Tales of the Trains*. (London: Downey and Co, 1899). p.95
9. Downey, *Charles Lever: His Life in His Letters*. I, p.325
10. Stevenson, *Dr Quicksilver*. p.197
11. *Ibid.* p.197
12. Tony Bareham, *Charles Lever: New Evaluations*. (Gerrards Cross: Colin Smythe, 1991) p.115
13. Lever, *The Dodd Family Abroad*. (London: Downey and Co, 1898) p.xii
14. Lever, *The Dodd Family Abroad*. (London: Routledge and Sons, n.d.) I, p.233
15. *Ibid.* I, pp.233–234
16. *Ibid.* I, p.360
17. Downey, *Charles Lever: His Life in His Letters*. I, p.321
18. *Ibid.* I, p.329
19. *Ibid.* I, p.329
20. Lever, *The Dodd Family Abroad*. I, p.72
21. *Ibid.* II, p.45
22. Stevenson, *Dr Quicksilver*. pp.197–8
23. Lever, *The Dodd Family Abroad*. I, p.310
24. Fitzpatrick, *The Life of Charles Lever*. p.283
25. Stevenson, *Dr Quicksilver*. p.197
26. *Ibid.* p.274
27. Downey, *Charles Lever: His Life in His Letters*. I, p.329
28. Bareham (ed.), *Charles Lever: New Evaluations*. p.109
29. Lever, *The Martins of Cro' Martin*. (London: Routledge and Sons, n.d.) I, p.15
30. *Ibid.* I, p.135
31. *Ibid.* II, p.46
32. Bareham (ed.), *Charles Lever: New Evaluations*. pp.14–15
33. Lever, *The Martins of Cro' Martin*. I, p.3
34. *Ibid.* I, p.159
35. *Ibid.* I, p.170
36. *Ibid.* I, p.124
37. *Ibid.* II, p.48
38. Stevenson, *Dr Quicksilver*. p.215
39. Lever, *The Martins of Cro' Martin*. II, p.71
40. *Ibid.* II, p. 295
41. Fitzpatrick, *The Life of Charles Lever*. p.312
42. Stevenson, *Dr Quicksilver*. pp.207–208
43. *Ibid.* p.215
44. Lever, *The Martins of Cro' Martin*. II, p.139
45. *Ibid.* I, p.9
46. *Ibid.* II, p.189
47. *Ibid.* I, p.28
48. *Ibid.* I, pp.107–118

49 *Ibid.* I, p.96
50 Bareham (ed.), *Charles Lever: New Evaluations.* pp.115–116

CHAPTER FIVE

THE ART OF BREVITY

1. Charles Lever, *Nuts and Nutcrackers.* (London: Downey and Co., 1899) p.122
2. W.J. Fitzpatrick, *The Life of Charles Lever.* (London: Ward, Lock, & Co., 1884) p.178
3. Lionel Stevenson, *Dr Quicksilver: The Life of Charles Lever.* (London: Chapman and Hall, 1939) p.106
4. *Ibid.* p.144
5. Lever, *Nuts and Nutcrackers.* p.122
6. Stevenson, *Dr Quicksilver.* p.142
7. Lever, *Nuts and Nutcrackers.* p.162
8. *Ibid.* pp.163–164
9. *Ibid.* p.172
10. *Ibid.* p.198
11. Stevenson, *Dr Quicksilver.* p.125
12. Lever, *Nuts and Nutcrackers.* p.186
13. *Ibid.* p.197
14. *Ibid.* p.114
15. *Ibid.* p.114
16. *Ibid.* p.253
17. *Ibid.* p.262
18. *Ibid.* pp.219–220
19. *Ibid.* pp.223–225
20. *Ibid.* pp.209–211
21. *Ibid.* pp.221–223
22. Stevenson, *Dr Quicksilver.* p.252
23. Fitzpatrick, *The Life of Charles Lever.* p.237
24. Stevenson, *Dr Quicksilver.* p.258
25. Charles Lever, *Cornelius O'Dowd.* (Edinburgh and London: William Blackwood & Sons, 1864–1865) III, p.173
26. *Ibid.* III, p.87
27. *Ibid.* I, pp.168–169
28. *Ibid.* I, pp.1–2
29. *Ibid.* I, pp.19–20
30. *Ibid.* I, p.12
31. *Ibid.* III, pp.258–259
32. *Ibid.* III, p.258
33. *Ibid.* III, pp.49–50
34. *Ibid.* III, p.139
35. *Ibid.* III, p.129
36. *Ibid.* III, p.135
37. *Ibid.* I, p.58

Notes 163

38 Tony Bareham (ed.), *Charles Lever: New Evaluations*. (Gerrards Cross: Colin Smythe, 1991) p.9
39 Stevenson, *Dr Quicksilver*. p.261
40 *Ibid.* p.254
41 Edmund Downey, *Charles Lever: His Life in His Letters*. (Edinburgh and London: William Blackwood & Sons, 1906). II, p.276

CHAPTER SIX

LEVER'S ANTI-HEROINES

1 Tony Bareham (ed.), *Charles Lever: New Evaluations*. (Gerrards Cross: Colin Smythe, 1991) p.102
2 Edmund Downey, *Charles Lever: His Life in His Letters*. (Edinburgh: William Blackwood and Sons, 1906) II, p.85
3 W.J. Fitzpatrick, *The Life of Charles Lever*. (London: Ward, Lock and Co., 1884) p.336
4 *Ibid.* p.336
5 Lionel Stevenson, *Dr Quicksilver: The Life of Charles Lever*. (London: Chapman and Hall, 1939) p.273
6 Bareham (ed.), *Charles Lever: New Evaluations.* p. 27
7 Downey, *Charles Lever: His Life in His Letters*. II, p.138
8 *Ibid.* II, p.161
9 *Ibid.* II, p.182
10 Bareham (ed.), *Charles Lever: New Evaluations.* p.112
11 Fitzpatrick, *The Life of Charles Lever.* p.336
12 Charles Lever, *Sir Brook Fossbrooke*. (London: Routledge and Sons, n.d.) p.55
13 *Ibid.* p.113
14 *Ibid.* p.113
15 *Ibid.* p.253
16 Downey, *Charles Lever: His Life in His Letters*. II, p.173
17 Lever, *Sir Brook Fossbrooke.* p.186
18 *Ibid.* p.293
19 *Ibid.* p.177
20 *Ibid.* p.471
21 *Ibid.* p.263
22 *Ibid.* p.419
23 *Ibid.* p.487
24 *Ibid.* p.488
25 Downey, *Charles Lever: His Life in His Letters*. II, p.206
26 Fitzpatrick, *The Life of Charles Lever.* p.339
27 Lever, *The Bramleighs of Bishop's Folly*. (London: Downey and Co, 1899) p.22
28 *Ibid.* pp.72–73
29 *Ibid.* p.131
30 *Ibid.* p.83
31 *Ibid.* p.224–225

32 *Ibid.* p.225
33 *Ibid.* p.215
34 *Ibid.* pp.30–31
35 *Ibid.* p.255
36 *Ibid.* pp.342–343
37 *Ibid.* p.519
38 Bareham (ed.), *Charles Lever: New Evaluations.* p.110
39 Lever, *The Bramleighs of Bishop's Folly.* pp.33–34
40 Fitzpatrick, *The Life of Charles Lever.* p.362
41 Bareham (ed.), *Charles Lever: New Evaluations.* pp.120–121
42 Lever, *Lord Kilgobbin.* p.364
43 *Ibid.* p.120
44 *Ibid.* p.99
45 *Ibid.* p.247
46 *Ibid.* p.365
47 *Ibid.* p.365
48 Lever, *That Boy of Norcott's.* (London: Routledge and Sons, n.d.) pp.180–181
49 Lever, *Lord Kilgobbin.* p.231
50 *Ibid.* p.231
51 *Ibid.* p.250
52 *Ibid.* p.255
53 *Ibid.* p.417

CHAPTER SEVEN

LAST EFFORTS

1 W.J. Fitzpatrick, *The Life of Charles Lever.* (London: Ward, Lock & Co., 1884) p.342
2 Lionel Stevenson, *Dr Quicksilver: The Life of Charles Lever.* (London: Chapman and Hall, 1939) p.283
3 *Ibid.* p.285
4 Fitzpatrick, *The Life of Charles Lever.* p.339
5 Charles Lever, *That Boy of Norcott's.* (London: Routledge and Sons, n.d.) p.23
6 *Ibid.* p.21
7 *Ibid.* p.55
8 *Ibid.* pp.180–181
9 *Ibid.* p.53
10 A.N. Jeffares, *Anglo-Irish Literature.* (Dublin: Gill and Macmillan, 1982) p.124
11 Charles Lever, *Lord Kilgobbin.* (Belfast: The Appletree Press, 1992) p.14
12 *Ibid.* pp.32–33
13 Georg Lukacs, *The Historical Novel.* (London: Penguin, 1981) p.59
14 Lever, *Lord Kilgobbin.* p.7
15 *Ibid.* p.8
16 *Ibid.* p.xii

17 *Ibid.* p.111
18 *Ibid.* pp.52–53
19 *Ibid.* p.425
20 *Ibid.* p.65
21 Lukacs, *The Historical Novel.* p.166
22 Lever, *Lord Kilgobbin.* p.66
23 *Ibid.* p.65
24 *Ibid.* p.22
25 *Ibid.* p.21
26 *Ibid.* p.128
27 *Ibid.* p.ix
28 *Ibid.* p.47
29 *Ibid.* p.134
30 *Ibid.* p.329
31 Fitzpatrick, *The Life of Charles Lever.* p.363
32 Lever, *Lord Kilgobbin.* p.xiii
33 *Ibid.* p.186
34 James M. Cahalan, *The Irish Novel, A Critical History.* (Dublin: Gill and Macmillan, 1988) p.70
35 Lever, *Lord Kilgobbin.* pp.141–142
36 *Ibid.* p.281
37 *Ibid.* p.199
38 Edmund Downey, *Charles Lever: His Life in His Letters.* (Edinburgh and London: William Blackwood and Sons, 1906). II, p.272
39 R.F. Foster (ed.), *The Oxford Illustrated History of Ireland.* (Oxford: Oxford University Press, 1989). p.207
40 Downey, *Charles Lever: His Life in His Letters.* II, p.325
41 Lever, *Lord Kilgobbin.* p.93
42 Lukacs, *The Historical Novel.* p.31

INDEX

References to the novels and stories of Charles Lever can be found under their individual titles

America, United States of 55
American Civil War 51
Appletree Press, Belfast 15
Arthur O'Leary 68
Athenaeum, The 100
Athens 147
Austria 94

Baden 94
Balzac, Honore de 14, 49
Bantry Bay 34, 57, 62
Bareham, Tony 22, 32, 36, 48, 90, 95, 97, 103, 115-116, 117, 119, 128, 135
Belgium 24, 28, 89, 94
Black Mask, The 68
Blackwood, John 88, 111, 112, 116, 118, 120, 152
Blake, William 25, 31
Boulogne 123
Boyne, Battle of the 143
Bramleighs of Bishop's Folly, The 28, 29, 34, 76, 118-119, 123-125, 134-135, 138
Bristol, Earl of 28
British Museum 46
Bronte, Charlotte *Jane Eyre* 139
Browne, Hablot K. (Phiz) 84
Browne, Sir Thomas 105-106; *Pseudoxia Epidemica* 105
Brussels 20, 32, 39, 49
Butt, Isaac 17

Cahalan, James M. 30, 33, 39, 44, 45, 150

Canada 24
Carleton, William 12, 24, 25, 27, 35, 39, 40, 53, 68, 69
Castlereagh, Lord 77-79
Catholic Emancipation 13
Catholic Emancipation Act (1829) 74, 75, 95, 102-103
Chapman and Hall, publishers 17, 32, 73, 111
Charles O'Malley, the Irish Dragoon 14, 15, 17, 20, 23, 24, 25, 28, 32, 39, 41, 45-51, 53-55, 67, 68, 91, 108, 138, 142
Charles X, of France 24, 99
Cholera 19, 27, 69, 71, 95, 101
Church of Ireland 22, 151, 152
Clare 19
Cockton, Henry *Valentine Vox the Ventriloquist* 46
Colburn and Bentley, publishers 34
College Green, Dublin 74
Collins, Wilkie 34
Con Cregan 94
Confessions of Harry Lorrequer, The 14, 17, 18, 21, 23, 24, 25, 27, 28, 32, 34, 39, 40-45, 47, 49, 54, 55, 67, 68, 91, 93, 108, 138, 153
Constable of Edinburgh, printers 11
Constantinople 147
Cooper, James Fennimore 49
Cork 43
Corkery, Daniel 26, 35; *Hidden Ireland, The* 26
Cornelius O'Dowd 105, 112, 115-116

County Down 29
Crane, Steven *Red Badge of Courage* 51
Crimean War 50
Cronin, Anthony 33, 43
Curran, John Philpot 29
Curry and Co, publishers 73

Daltons, The 11, 94
Davis, Thomas 19
Defenderism 58
Dickens, Charles 12, 17, 18, 32, 35, 40, 52, 53, 64, 69; *Bleak House* 95; *Old Curiosity Shop, The* 33; *Pickwick Papers, The* 17, 69
Dictionary of National Biography 27, 34
Dodd Family Abroad, The 24, 68, 87-89, 91-95, 107, 111, 141
Donleavy, J.P. 45
Downey and Company, publishers 11, 15
Downey, Edmund 15, 19, 42
Downhill 28
Dublin 70, 98
Dublin Castle 14, 64
Dublin University Magazine, The 17, 22, 23, 40, 67, 73, 105-106, 108, 112

Edgeworth, Maria 18, 20, 21, 32, 43, 63, 68, 131, 144, 148; *Absentee, The* 148; *Castle Rackrent* 18, 43, 59; *Ennui* 21, 148
Eliot, George 35; *Middlemarch* 33
Encumbered Estates Court 28

Fenians 13, 22, 36, 132, 148, 149-151
Fitzpatrick, W.J. 15, 45, 89, 94, 106, 111, 118, 123, 124, 138
Florence 51
Fortunes of Glencore, The 34
Foster, R.F. 20, 22, 24, 26, 30, 37, 71, 74, 151
France 89

Gaelic League 26
Galway 52, 89
Germany 24, 94
Gladstone, William Ewart 13, 36, 151-152
Glenflesk, Valley of 65
Gothic fiction 48
Grafton Street, Dublin 46, 47

Hall, Samuel Carter 108
Haslam, Richard 70
Home Rule 22
House of Lords 110

Italy 24, 94

Jack Hinton, the Guardsman 11, 21, 148
James II 143
James, G.P.R. 32
James, M.R. 19
Jeffares, A. Norman 20, 24, 30, 64, 118, 141, 144, 147, 149, 152
Joyce, James 30, 33

Kiberd, Declan 25
Kipling, Rudyard 52
Knight of Gwynne, The 17, 18, 34, 71, 73, 74, 75, 81, 83-85, 87, 95

Lamb, Charles 112-113
Land Act (1870) 152
Le Fanu, Joseph Sheridan 19, 35
Lever, James 19
London 23
Lord Kilgobbin 13, 15, 20, 21, 22, 24, 25, 29, 30, 31, 36, 44, 64, 65, 67, 82, 108, 117, 119, 129, 135, 137, 141, 143-145, 148-153
Louise XIV, of France 100
Louis-Philippe, of France 100
Lover, Samuel 25, 27, 41
Low Countries 61
Lukacs, Georg 20, 143, 145

Index

Lytton, Edward Bulwer- *Last Days of Pompeii* 33

M'Glashan, James 55, 63, 68, 73, 138
Macauley, Thomas 31
Martin, Mary Letitia 28
Martins of Cro' Martin, The 13, 20, 24, 27, 28, 29, 30, 36, 71, 74, 81, 87, 88, 92, 95-96, 100-103, 117, 143, 152
Marx, Karl 26, 27
Maturin, Charles 132
Maxwell, William Hamilton *Fortunes of Hector Halloran, The* 50
Mayne, Commissary-General 52
Messines, Battle of 50
Moore, Thomas 29
Morash, Chris 25, 28, 30, 65
Munich 23, 42

Nation, The 68, 69
Normanby, Lord 107
Northern Ireland 37
Nuts and Nutcrackers 22, 89, 105-106, 109-112, 115-116

O'Brien, Flann 45
O'Connell, Daniel 13, 31, 36, 75, 80, 81, 102, 106, 110
O'Donoghue, The 19, 21, 22, 29, 30, 34, 57, 58, 63, 64, 65, 67-69, 73, 87, 108, 110, 117, 151
O'Faolain, Sean 33
Observer, The 27
Ouida 14
Owenson, Sydney - Lady Morgan 20, 131

Paris 99, 100
Paul and Virginia 138
Peninsula Campaigns 23, 48, 49, 50
Phoenix Park, Dublin 107
Poe, Edgar Allen 55
Portstewart 28

Protestant Ascendancy 13, 14, 19, 20, 26, 29, 35, 36, 39, 57, 74, 75, 80, 81, 83, 99, 103, 142, 150, 152

Rackrenting 59, 80, 96, 98, 142
Repeal 67, 80, 106
Reynolds, Lorna 53, 54
Ribbonmen 145
Ritchie, Lady 51
Roland Cashel 28, 34, 108
Rossa, Jeremiah O'Donovan 149
Routledge and Sons, publishers 15
RTE 25

Saintsbury, George 25
Savage Landor, Walter 46
Scotland 109
Scott, Sir Walter 14, 20, 30, 31, 49, 143, 152
Shakespeare, William 25, 31
Shaw, George Bernard 23
Sir Brook Fossbrooke 29, 30, 48, 63, 88, 114, 117-119, 123-125, 134-135
Sir Jasper Carew 89
Sloan, Barry 40, 44, 54, 58, 59
Somerville and Ross 41
Spencer, Alexander 34, 68, 92
Spenser, Edmund 25
Spezzia 64, 137
St Patrick's Eve 13, 19, 20, 27, 41, 57, 69-71, 83, 85, 87, 95, 100-101, 110, 143, 152
Stevenson, Lionel 15, 28, 49, 55, 85, 88, 90, 91, 94, 99, 100, 106, 111, 137
Surtees, R.S. 14
Sutherland, J.A. 17, 18, 32, 33, 73, 84
Synge, J.M. 20

Tales of the Trains 89
Talleyrand 47
Templeogue House 23
Thackeray, William Makepeace 12, 17, 23, 27, 28, 35, 51, 69; *Irish Sketchbook, The* 23; *Pendennis* 28;

Vanity Fair 129
That Boy of Norcott's 31, 131, 137-138, 140
Tom Burke of Ours 34
Trieste 41, 64, 137
Trinity College, Dublin 19, 45, 46, 52, 115
Trollope, Anthony 24, 32, 33, 34, 35; *Autobiography* 25
Trollope, Frances *Old World and the New, The* 51
Tuileries 100
Tyrone 12

Ulster Presbyterianism 58
Union, Act of (1800) 70-71, 73-76, 79, 80, 83-85, 95, 98
United Irishmen 58, 61, 62, 151

Victoria, Queen 109

Waterloo, Battle of 48, 49, 51
Wellington, Duke of 52
Westminster 64, 74
Whigs 106, 124, 150, 151
Whist 32, 94, 113
Whiteboys 145
Whyte-Melville, George John *Interpreter, The* 50
Wordsworth, William 30; *Excursion, The* 31
World War I 50
World War II 94

Yeats, W.B. 24, 26, 39
Young Irishmen 74